Limitless You

HOLLY WYNN

**ACTIVATE YOUR SOUL, GET OUT OF YOUR FUNK
AND START LIVING YOUR BEST LIFE**

LIMITLESS *You*

NEW YORK

LONDON • NASHVILLE • MELBOURNE • VANCOUVER

Limitless You

Activate Your Soul, Get Out of Your Funk and Start Living Your Best Life

Published in New York, New York, by Morgan James Publishing. Morgan James is a trademark of Morgan James, LLC. www.MorganJamesPublishing.com

Proudly distributed by Publishers Group West®

Morgan James BOGO™

A **FREE** ebook edition is available for you or a friend with the purchase of this print book.

[ ]

CLEARLY SIGN YOUR NAME ABOVE

Instructions to claim your free ebook edition:
1. Visit MorganJamesBOGO.com
2. Sign your name CLEARLY in the space above
3. Complete the form and submit a photo of this entire page
4. You or your friend can download the ebook to your preferred device

ISBN 9781636981154 paperback
ISBN 9781636981161 ebook
Library of Congress Control Number:
2022951280

Cover & Interior Design by:
Christopher Kirk
www.GFSstudio.com

Morgan James PUBLISHING

Builds

with...
Habitat for Humanity®
Peninsula and Greater Williamsburg

Morgan James is a proud partner of Habitat for Humanity Peninsula and Greater Williamsburg. Partners in building since 2006.

Get involved today! Visit: www.morgan-james-publishing.com/giving-back

Dedication

To anyone who is in their personal discovery process
—I'm rooting for you.

Table of Contents

Dear Reader,

Let me be honest. When I started writing this book, my first thought was, "Oh my gosh, this is huge," and it made me nervous. I'm experiencing a moment in time when I'm at a point of choice. What does that mean, exactly? Well, it's a time in your life when you are about to expand into a different version of yourself. You're pushing forward from what you consider to be just a part of your ordinary life into the unknown. You can feel that you're at a threshold and about to step through into a new reality.

I've heard people call it whispers from the soul, but for me, it's more like a soul nudge because some movement is required. You can feel it speaking to you, beckoning you onto this new path with outcomes that your mind can't understand, but you feel it, and you just know you need to act. It is time to ignite those feeling senses deep within you.

You aren't reading your average flowery holistic self-help book. I won't lie and tell you that from this moment on, you'll be dancing around in fields of daisies for the rest of your life. Right now, I'm going from pretty darn good to even better. That hasn't always been the case. I had the same kind of soul nudge when I was in a dark place. I was inundated and weighed down with so many beliefs and past hurts that didn't serve me anymore. I felt like I'd lost myself.

Sometimes people at that darker point of choice hear their inner voice saying things like, "I can't live like this anymore." It can be confusing. It's not that you've done something wrong or you've brought all kinds of awful things into your life, and now you're being punished. It's not that your life is hopeless, and you'd be better off leaving this world altogether. It's a place where you are ready to learn how to set down all of those heavy feelings that have expired and move forward into a different reality that contains new thoughts and beliefs that will align with the person you were born to become.

Thank God that soul nudge for me was more like, "I'm not going out like this." I remember looking in the mirror at myself and thinking, "Who in the world is that woman?" It was such a low moment, but I know it's when I was finally ready to move forward toward something different.

Throughout life, we experience trauma and cope with it in so many different ways.

I've had what people might consider more than my fair share of trauma in mine. I even had a high school friend ask me if my family was cursed, and I found myself considering that thought as the truth at one point.

I wondered if there was a connection between all of the heart attacks in the older generation of my family and the heartbreaking loss they'd suffered as young adults themselves. I wondered how my grandparents could be the life of the parties at their lake house and successful business owners while being so emotionally distant from their children at home.

I thought about my aunt a lot. I remember seeing her looking out her window at my house across the street, and I'd wonder, "What's her deal?" She intrigued me, but I was ill-equipped to understand enough to help her fully at such a young age. It would rip me to pieces, thinking about how sad and lonely she must be, but I just knew that it would hurt her even more if I brought it up, and I couldn't do that to her. So, I kept it to myself.

I considered my other aunt, a Southern beauty queen, gone before I was born. And my college-aged dad's somber response to my future mama when he heard the news that his sister was gone, "At least she finally got the peace she wanted."

What was ailing my aunt in the prime of her life? How did this beauty queen who seemingly had it all feel like her only path to peace was leaving this world? I spent countless days as a young teen searching for the note my dad left behind after I finally heard the truth about his accident that occurred when I was six.

My brothers and I went to a psychologist when we were young, and I made it my life-long mission to study psychology. While I tried to figure out my lost friends and family members, I realized that I learned how to understand so much about who I am and why I lived the way I did.

There was so much heavy-hearted information for me to process. I needed answers because I just couldn't live in a world where dads would just check out and take their lives. I couldn't live in a world where that was just how things were. I wanted to help people before they decided it was better to leave this world.

I worked in a clinic and felt a calling to do something a little more on the untraditional side of things, which led me to work one-on-one with clients to help them live more fully and become the most accurate versions of themselves.

Maybe right now you're feeling pulled between your ordinary life and an extraordinarily enhanced life that your mind can't fully grasp the possibility of. What you need is a collaboration between your mind, heart, and soul. I'm here to tell you this is possible for anyone. No matter where you are right now, it's time to dig deep and bring out your truest self.

People always ask me what it takes to come up with the courage to live their truth.

Throughout life, we collect programming along the way that causes us to shut down our voices, or even shut them off entirely. When you uncover the true essence inside yourself, you open up the realm of possibilities when you honor your truth, speak it out loud, and start to live a life that reflects it.

So many people shy away from this idea because we feel like speaking up may hurt another loved one, offend someone, or come across as selfish. The fear that others view or perceive us in a certain way is often a motivating force as we interact with others, choose our dialogue, or even take action. Every time we fall into this way of thinking, we cause a slight disruption in the harmony of our energy, boundaries, and most importantly, our alignment.

When you speak or live in a way that doesn't totally align with your truth or your alignment, you create unnecessary suffering or self-criticism that results in unpreferred emotions and feelings. Eventually, you begin to veer off the path that was meant for you from the beginning of your life. You start to feel unsure about yourself and the things that you truly value.

Sometimes you have to release your need to control the outcome or situation and lovingly, kindly speak your truth. That way you can honor your boundaries, your soul, and your heart while also honoring those around you by showing them it's okay to be exactly who you are.

I implore you to consider a few things you can do each day that allow you to speak your truth in a loving manner. Just because you speak your truth doesn't mean you have to blatantly disregard others in an aggressive or rude manner. It simply means that you find the balance to speak your truth from your heart that feels fully aligned.

It is time for real-life applications.

Yes, I'm here to inspire you and equip you with the necessary tools to bring you into a different life. But I've also been in those dark places. If you get to a quote that irritates you to no end, or you don't understand how it makes sense for where you are right now, I get it. But I need you to feel that feeling, acknowledge it, and then give yourself the time to keep reading and trust that it's setting up your point of growth.

As you move forward, I would love for you to consider taking notes (audio or written) as you read. When something you've read resonates with you, make a note of it. Take the time to explore the feeling behind the thought. And as you reach the end of each chapter, I'd like to encourage you to actively participate with the questions and suggestions. I'm inviting you to read the chapters and then have a way to process the information, so it sticks with you after you put the book down.

It's time to trust your growth and open your mind and heart to access some different parts of yourself. Feeling uncomfortable or awkward makes perfect sense. Trust that those feelings are there because you're on your way towards new growth. In those moments, I ask for your courage and your willingness to grow into your truest self. Consider reading my book as an investment in you. Trust your growth process and appreciate this new journey to move out of your comfort zone and into your best life, and you'll be amazed by where you end up!

I'd like to consider this book as my offering to all the family members in my life who were gone before their time and to those of you reading this who feel like you're lost right now. Feeling lost doesn't necessarily mean that you are in the depths of despair (though you may be).

You may feel lost even when you experience a lot of success and receive all kinds of validation and accolades from the world around you. Your world looks impressive. But in those quiet moments when you're honest with yourself, there's a hole you can't quite fill. It's a silent yearning for something more. I hope you felt led to join me here and find your way back to what makes you feel the most alive.

I've followed my heart, and it led me to this place. I trust that now is the perfect time to share my thoughts and experiences to help you find your way back to life. I am here to tell you if I can live through so much and make it to the other side, so can you. It's not too late. It is my great hope that we've found each other for a divine purpose and a very specific reason. So, let's lock arms and do this!

I love psychology and getting deep into all the whys and the hows. Keep an eye out for little sprinkles of science as you go. For now, just consider listening to my Georgia-grown Southern drawl as I say, you only know whatcha know when you know it!

And now is the perfect time to get back to you.

Love and Light to you all,
Holly

You deserve an intimate connection
with yourself.

#LimitlessYou

What is a Soul, Anyways?

*What is a soul? It's like electricity—we don't really
know what it is, but it's a force that can light a room.*
~ Ray Charles

When I consider this question, what immediately comes to mind is that the soul is the *you*. Your soul knows everything about the truest version of who you are. It isn't filtered through anyone else's opinions, projections, perceptions, expectations, beliefs, or ideas whatsoever. It is literally that quiet space inside of you that if you can sink deep enough into, you can hear the truth of who you actually are.

It's also the space where we remind ourselves of our divine connection to all that is. Whether you're an atheist or consider yourself religious or spiritual, we're still light particles from places beyond us. You aren't just this body that happened to sprout into action on planet Earth. We really come from a miraculous beginning.

I mean, think about the human gestation process. We're all little walking miracles! And your soul activates your body and allows it to be. The soul's expression is interpreted as the body in motion. We're not here to live life as we process it through the thoughts and beliefs of other people around us, and that's where we get tricked and fall into the traps of this life.

We aren't supposed to come here and live our lives through someone else's filter. But as we grow older, we have this tendency to move away from our soul's purpose, sometimes to the point where we can't hear it anymore. That's when we start to feel confused, irritable, and like something's missing but we can't quite figure out what it is.

We need to distinguish between that quiet space inside that leads us to understand and experience life while we coexist with the people around us. When we put too much emphasis outside of ourselves, that's when we become susceptible to the mind's tricks and traps. We start to believe we're only what someone else thinks we should be, or even worse, we try to fit ourselves into a definition of who we are not.

Your soul space is that inner truth. If you meditate and get into that space, you may only feel the stillness and hear nothing but silence. This is actually a great place to be because it shows that you possess the ability to take yourself away from that constant chatter that we tend to be surrounded by daily. Everyone else's everything sort of falls away, and you're left with the clarity of understanding your most authentic self.

Tapping into your soul space also allows you to see the one-ness of all that exists on our planet. You can look at the breeze rippling through leaves in a tree and see the beauty in those little everyday occurrences. You give yourself permission to see the beauty in the little things and find a sense of peace and gratitude from within.

I tend to find my soul space in the silliest things. Even just driving down the street and looking at one of those huge restaurant signs takes me into such a beautiful space of wonder. It's a reminder of the miracle of human potential. Follow along with me here.

So, I look up at a sign and start thinking:

- It's so cool that someone came up with this idea, and now we can find that sign all over the world.
- Someone came up with this symbol, and it has become the representation of all the food that the people within the restaurant create, calling out to everyone.
- Someone else figured out how to create a sign that people could see from a distance and that could light up at night without catching on fire.
- Then there had to be someone else who created a machine that could lift the sign into the air.
- And yet another person showed up who knew how to create the post it would sit on so it wouldn't topple to the ground.

It makes me believe how powerful our souls can be when we align our truest intentions and desires with our potential, let go of the fear of the unknown, and chase after the idea that showed up on our heart one day.

Sometimes we are misled into thinking that we have to do something that is service based to make an impact on the world. But that isn't the case. We're all guilty of going with the flow of society at some point and losing pieces of our individuality. When each of us can tap into our soul and become who we were meant to be, it creates a ripple effect of inspiration. When we can live from a place of being aligned with our souls, everyone can appreciate each other's most genuine gifts and abilities.

The need to compare yourself to others melts away. You don't worry about being seen or judged by anyone else. You are just you, and they are just them. And we're all here to live our best lives while supporting each other. How amazing would that be if everyone could live fully aligned to their soul?

What does it mean to be in alignment with ourselves? Great question!

Your alignment is the internal barometer that helps you understand what is true and living within. You can also think of it as a guiding light that gives you a clearer path to navigate life.

When your personality wants to attach to an idea, hold on, or have all the answers backed up with a story, that's coming from an imbalanced ego. It wants to justify actions, stand in defensiveness, and claim victimhood.

Your soul is in constant connection with God/Source. It trusts and surrenders to knowing that life isn't a big test or a way to earn worthiness. So, when you can regain your equilibrium, you can allow the understanding that experiences occur to open you up to change.

You can choose to observe those changes in life through neutrality without the need to attach to any story or pattern if you can remain congruent to your alignment. There is no need to attach to any story because the soul is forever present. You only attach yourself to stories, circumstances, outcomes, and people from a pressing need.

So, when your personality begins to insert insecurities and demands, you tend to feed it by consuming the information that confirms how it feels. Ever heard the phrase misery loves company? This happens to all of us at some point. We watch the programs and news that confirm our fears. We talk to others in the voice of those fears rather than from our truth. We rope other people into our stories instead of claiming the space for solutions.

And then those patterns that don't serve you start to show up. You find yourself:

- Staying busy without accomplishing much.
- Procrastinating.
- Eating foods that lower your vibe.
- Doing things in excess.
- Shutting down.
- Turning to substances that override your ability to feel your soul.

But when you tune into your soul space and therefore your alignment, you can surrender to higher opportunities and possibilities. You start to open up instead of shutting down. You begin to feel your connection to God/Source strengthening, and it feels safe to let go and allow new opportunities for growth and expansion to appear.

It's vital to understand your inner world before you can demonstrate your truth to the outer world. Try these reflection points:

- Get honest with yourself about your emotional state, attitude, and feelings. Don't suppress, shame yourself, or deny what you notice in that moment. Observe them through a lens of curiosity and love for yourself.
- When you're watching yourself in a time of struggle or strife, activate observance and acceptance. Get curious about why you react or behave in a specific way, and try to understand yourself without placing guilt or shame into that new awareness.
- Communicate your feelings and thoughts from a place of honor (for yourself and others) without fearing how others may receive you and without suppressing or spewing them indiscriminately.
- Notice and explore your attachments and the intentions that are behind them. You can discover blocks and limitations that hold you back.
- Say yes to your truth by saying no to mistreatment, feeling used, or appeasing someone else out of obligation, guilt, or shame.

- Create healthy boundaries that honor your physical, emotional, and mental well-being while supporting the foundation of your wholeness.
- Adopt the affirmation, "It is safe to be me. All of me. Forever me."

If that list isn't resonating with you just yet, don't worry. Go ahead and mark this page to revisit later and look at it through your new understanding. As you move through this journey, we'll keep working on strengthening your inner world.

So, now you know my definitions of the soul and alignment, but how do you actually start to activate your soul? If you've lived so long as someone else's definition of who you are, how do you get back to the truest version of yourself?

It all starts with vulnerability.

Being vulnerable isn't a sign of weakness. It's the best way for you to get real and raw with yourself, and as a result, you can process and let go of those thoughts and feelings that don't serve you anymore.

Here's the thing: a lot of times, when you think about sitting quietly and listening to yourself, you already know what you're going to hear from within, and it isn't all love and light and glitter and rainbows, right? We want to keep ourselves busy. We want to keep ourselves stimulated. We want to keep ourselves distracted from those inner thoughts, and we *never* want to feel bored.

Because if we sit quietly that voice will get loud, and it isn't actually your soul's voice. This is where so many people get confused. If you sit with your thoughts long enough, you start to hear those old tricks and traps.

- I'm not good enough.
- I'm not loved.
- I'm not worthy.
- I'm stupid.

Instead of throwing your hands in the air and saying, "Welp, that just made me feel awful! Forget quiet time. This is absolutely horrible! Why would anyone want to do this on purpose?" give those negative thoughts some airtime. They are popping up for a reason, and if you can think back to the places where they originated and start to remind yourself that they aren't your thoughts, you'll begin to reconnect with your soul.

Is vulnerability easy? Absolutely not! I guarantee that the first time you make a list of the thoughts that pop up, it's going to be uncomfortable. Maybe even a little heartbreaking.

But when you disagree with those negative thoughts and send your retriever brain out to find counterexamples, those thoughts won't be so loud the next time you get quiet. And eventually, they won't be there anymore! Let me say that again! Eventually those negative thoughts won't exist in your mind once you understand how to release them. Doesn't that sound amazing?

Processing these emotions that had a lot of power at one time in your life is a difficult thing. Maybe you're scared to face them. Perhaps you're unsure of how to approach them, but if you allow your soul space to connect with your mind, heart, and body, then you can integrate those energies and feel more confident from within.

Your next step to activate your soul is meditation. But first, let's get nerdy!

Meditation helps you not only to "quiet your mind" as you hear all the time, but it allows you to process your emotions from a biological standpoint. When you go into meditation, you essentially neutralize your nervous system. You aren't as overstimulated, and all the frantic energy on the surface can settle down.

When you take the time to soothe your nervous system, your parasympathetic nervous system is activated. When you put yourself into that settled state of being, you can move away from the surface-level stuff that was never yours to begin with. Then you can really start to differentiate between your own energy, thoughts, and feelings versus those that came along for the ride due to an experience or what someone else told you to be true.

Not sure where to start with meditation? No worries! I've got a chapter dedicated to creating your practice with the steps I used!

Okay, Holly, so to activate my soul, I choose to allow myself to be vulnerable and then start working on a meditation practice. Let's say I'm good with both of those, and I begin to connect more with my inner world. How do I know it's really a soul nudge that I should listen to and not another trick or trap in my mind?

Well, that thought or feeling came from somewhere. But you need to be able to use your awareness to pinpoint exactly where it originated. Did you feel it in your gut? Was it coming from your heart? Or were you frantically trying to find the solution to something?

It made no logical sense when I felt the soul nudge to take a job in a different state. I was a single mom. We had just lost my brother and were grieving. I didn't want to leave my mom and make her feel like I was abandoning her, but I just *knew* it was the right thing to do. There was no evidence to prove my feelings. It just came from somewhere deep inside of me. In my soul.

When you feel that soul nudge and you pull it out to the surface, what do you do with it? As humans, we have a natural impulse to turn on our little retriever brain and send it out to look for clues. Then we ask other people to add their logic and what their brains have shown them over time, which oftentimes can lead us astray.

It's almost as though you take the pure little prompt from your soul, put it into a pot, and add a little water. Then you take it to your sister's house, and she tosses in a rock. Your next stop is to your friend's house, and she lovingly adds a handful of her own rocks. Bring it up at work, and the pot's so dang heavy you just set it down and try to forget about it. But trust me, your subconscious won't let it go.

There is a difference between asking for participation and asking for permission. Getting someone's advice or asking for their support doesn't mean they get to tell you that you can or cannot move forward. Ultimately, the decision is yours to make.

The next time you feel that little soul nudge:

- Write it down as soon as you can. What did you hear? Where did it feel like it originated?
- It's a precious gift that could change the trajectory of your life, so treat it as such.

- Honor yourself enough to sit with it and allow yourself the ability to make your decision from your own place of power.

Try this:

You'll want to share your soul's nudge with other people. It's just human nature. But before you take it to someone else, ask yourself:

- Whose voice do I really want to involve in my decision-making process?
- Whose opinion is one that I genuinely trust?
- Who has been a great listener for me in the past?
- Do I really need someone's permission to move forward?

Consider this:

- Some decisions affect other people, but you can still honor your soul when you bring up the discussion.
- If you want to truly live aligned to your soul, you need to listen to yourself.
- When in doubt, remind others, "I'm not doing this *to you*. I'm doing it *for me*."

The more you connect with your soul, the more you remain in contact with what is true and purposeful in your life. It's time to believe that you *are* capable of loving yourself as the perfect imperfection you are. It's important to grant yourself the time to find your inner alignment. Being here with me is a great first step! Keep going!

Did you: Speak your truth? Honor your heart?
Honor yourself? Honor your emotions?
Honor your body? Honor your energy?

#LimitlessYou

Lean in and Love Yourself.

*One way to feel good about yourself is to love
yourself...to take care of yourself.*
~ Goldie Hawn

You've heard it from other thought leaders, and you'll hear it from me, too. Lean in. Let me tell you. I was very unfamiliar with this concept at the beginning of my personal development journey. That phrase kept popping up. Lean in. And I'm like, what in the world are you saying? What does that even *mean?*

If you plan to address your soul nudges, meditate, trust your intuition, and heal, it's essential to understand this concept and how it applies to you. Here we go!

Think about a time when you were around a lot of people. Maybe a crowded restaurant or a big gathering with friends or family. You're having a conversation with someone, and there's noise all around. You want to hear what they're saying, so you physically lean in towards that person so that you can focus better.

Say you've got that friend in front of you. They're saying, "Oh, I feel so weak. I feel so disappointed in myself. I feel so defeated. I feel so sad. I feel so stupid. I can't believe I made this choice. I can't believe I did this thing."

You're going to get closer to them and see how you can be attentive to their needs. You may even scoop them up in a hug because you're like, "Whatever it takes, I'm here!"

Imagine that friend knocking on your door, showing up, and saying, "I need help. I can't believe I made this decision." Do you roll your eyes, tell them to quit being such a baby, and slam the door in their face?

Of course not!

You're also not going to worry about all those less critical thoughts at that time, right? You're going to tune into them completely. You won't ask if you can talk to them later because you're in the middle of a movie on Netflix. You're not going to worry about the phone ringing in the background. At this moment in time, you are the only two people in the world. You're going to focus solely on your friend, sharing your nurturing side with them.

You automatically ask yourself, what does this individual need right now? You may even subconsciously put your hand on your heart as they talk because you genuinely care about them, and you don't want to see them hurting.

Instead of leaning in as a way to help someone else, you lean in to focus on what you hear internally, and choose to listen, and then take action. That's what I'm asking you to do for yourself.

Lean in. Focus on what your soul is telling you.

This is the epitome of self-care.

Somewhere along the way, the idea of self-care got a little warped. When you hear the phrase self-care, do you automatically get the vision of a woman in a white robe lounging on the couch and eating bonbons? Or taking a luxurious trip to bask in the sun for weeks at a time?

Somehow, the difference between indulgence and self-care has blurred together. So many clients of mine thought if they were a girlfriend, wife, mother, or had a job, all of those people and to-do lists had to come before themselves. It's a belief passed to them from previous generations of women, telling them that the best of us put ourselves last.

But when you think about it, that idea makes absolutely no dang sense! If you put everyone and everything ahead of yourself, you simply cannot be the best version of yourself. How in the world do you expect to have all of the love and energy to give when there's nothing left for you at the end of the day?

Instead, let's focus on prioritizing your needs first. And when you feel filled to overflowing, you can share that with everyone and everything else that needs your attention without pouring yourself out and running on empty. See the difference?

It's not about getting your manicures, pedicures, and massages on. Those are things that I certainly love to do. There is a time and a place for those kinds of activities. However, with self-care, the very basis and foundation are leaning in, listening to, and nurturing yourself.

Self-care is also the opposite of resistance. Have you ever

heard someone say what you resist persists? If you are dealing with something bothersome, the worst thing you can do is ignore it. It's time to lean in so you can explore it and understand why it's even in your life.

Those things are showing up so we can understand, overcome, move through, and release. And that's how we move closer toward healing from within.

What does that version of you need that is either in pain, hurting, confused and lost, or regretting the past? And what steps can you take to meet those needs?

You don't discard it, and you don't kick it to the curb, and you certainly don't say mean things to yourself and shove those feelings down!

You lean in and say, what can I do for you right now? It's not an enabling feature. I'm not suggesting that you allow yourself to fall into the trap that life is just supposed to make us all victims. It's genuinely about transcending that lower experience into something more fruitful and meaningful.

If you lean in first, this is how you're also going to become a master of meditation because you're more equipped to figure out how to go about dealing with whatever is coming up during your meditation process. I know understanding how to lean in for myself would have helped me before I tried meditating because I was scared to death to sit with myself and listen to my own needs.

But when you understand how to lean in for yourself the same way you've done for others, you're ready to start your meditation practice, knowing that you feel equipped to take care of yourself when annoying things happen to show themselves to you!

Time for some journaling!

- Write about a time when you leaned in towards a friend who was going through a hard time.
- What was happening with them?
- What needs did you identify?
- How did you show them that you cared about their situation?

Try this:

When a friend needs help, you do whatever you can to help ease their pain. It's time to be the same kind of friend to *yourself*! The next time a need for self-care pops up, ask yourself:

- What are the thoughts and feelings that are present at this moment?
- What are the needs connected to them?
- How can I show myself that I care?
- Are the words I'm telling myself at this moment helping me or causing more pain?
- What is something that would make me feel better? Then take action!

Consider this:

- Taking the time for self-care is not selfish.
- When you nurture your soul, you love yourself.

When you choose to love yourself, it becomes easier to love others.

It's time to be your most important priority.
Trust me. It's worth it.

#LimitlessYou

You Can Meditate—I Promise!

Meditation makes the entire nervous system
go into a field of coherence.
~ Deepak Chopra

S ome people think meditation is a pointless activity or a waste of time. Others may think it's only for a group of monks sitting on the side of a mountain who have all taken a vow of silence. Going into a quiet, dark space with your own mind can seem terrifying for someone victimized or traumatized. The idea of stillness can freak you out even if you haven't had really bad things happen in your life.

Let's face it. We are programmed to be in a constant state of busyness. No one wants to be bored. But get this! When we're bored, we actually have the time to learn more about ourselves. And we know that facing and shifting away from those unwanted and false thoughts is often an uncomfortable process.

But it's hard for so many people (including myself when I started) to figure out how to be quiet and still when most of our waking life has our eyeballs glued to a screen. Do you know what I mean? It's no wonder that when you are used to having a screen in your face for around twelve hours a day, and then I ask you to sit quietly in the dark for thirty minutes, your brain starts to tell you it's impossible. It really does mirror a withdrawal symptom!

What happens in your mind when you choose to leave your comfort zone and expose yourself to new experiences? It's time to get curious about the way your body is responding to external and internal stimuli. If your brain perceives anything new as a threat, it wants to take you into a place of fight, flight, faint, or freeze. You don't have to see a tiger charging at you for it to activate. Anything out of your comfort zone can signal your amygdala that a threat is on its way, and you need to choose one of those "f-words" listed above to survive!

Most people are familiar with fight or flight, the two most common "f-words". Fight can mean a verbal argument as well as a physical fight. Flight wants to keep you safe by removing you from the situation. You feel an urge to leave the room, or you may inwardly retreat. Faint could represent literally fainting in a stressful moment, or maybe you just start to feel fatigue and need a nap. Freeze could show up as the inability to physically move from where you stand, or you could lock yourself in a space of indecision instead.

Time for some science!

How can you disarm your brain to the point where you can get started on a meditation practice without hearing that inner critic screaming that you should give up before you try and fail miserably? In the same way, you're going to move out of your comfort zone over and over along this journey. The answer lies in working with your parasympathetic nervous system.

Your parasympathetic nervous system is the part of your brain that regulates your sense of stability and calms you down. Any time you try to sit down and meditate (or leave your comfort zone and try anything new, for that matter), you don't want to feel fragmented. For example, maybe you've been attempting to force yourself to concentrate on something, but your hand is tapping the table, and your mind is thinking about dinner and the grocery list. Let's get your mind, body, and soul on the same page so you can try this first new thing—meditation.

The vagus nerve is the most influential of all nerves in your parasympathetic nervous system. I like to think of it as your body's natural reset button. If you can consciously stimulate it, you will bring about more and more calm and collected feelings. It brings a greater sense of success and expands your comfort zone as you learn and grow.

When you're stimulating that vagus nerve, it sends messages to all of your organs and helps them to relax and settle down, too. If you're constantly communicating the same messages throughout your body, you're creating internal traffic jams. Most of this traffic sends messages from the body to the brain.

As the vagus nerve communicates with your parasympathetic nervous system it can bring forth feelings of:

- Stability
- Calm
- Confidence
- Emotional Stability
- Regulated blood sugar
- Resilience
- Longevity

The higher your vagal tone is, the greater the difference in your heart rate as you breathe in compared to when you breathe out. This strengthens your state of relaxation.

The lower the tone is, the more you feel the impact in the form of:

- Low energy
- Instability in your mood
- Chronic fatigue
- Chronic inflammation
- Heart issues

To stimulate the vagus nerve and activate your parasympathetic nervous system, you want to focus on activities that are soothing. And that is why I'm sprinkling in the science here. Meditation is an amazing way to slow down and relax throughout your journey of transformation.

Have you ever gone to a yoga class or seen one on television where the people sit together and say, Ommmmmm? Stimulating your vocal cords also activates your vagus nerve. Think about it. The vibration of that long and slow sound spreads throughout your body and causes a response within your parasympathetic nervous system, which regulates your heartbeat and your breath. You become more unified at that moment.

Now that you have the scientific backup, let's talk about meditation.

I don't naturally sit still very well. I'm one of those people who is over-analyzing all the time. And I'll be honest, the first time I tried a group meditation, I thought for a minute that my brain might just implode!

The meditation leader talked about envisioning a rose as you saw yourself sitting in the middle of your head. And we were supposed to use that rose to tidy up our space. You know, kind of look around our heads and clean out the useless dust sitting around.

Sounds impressive, doesn't it? It sounds so beautiful and enlightening, it makes you think you're about to hear the story of what I saw and how amazing I felt, right? Wrong! Here's the truth about what it sounded like in my head:

I'm feeling quiet. Wait. Am I quiet? Yes, I feel quiet now. Am I going to see something in my head, or is it just going to stay like this dark void? Oh, I think I see something! What do I see? Wait, there's a rose! Can I see a rose? I don't know! It's over to the left. Okay, I have to look over to the left. Oh no! It's gone. Now I can't even see the stinking rose, and I'm supposed to be swirling it around. Welp, it's gone. My brain's too cluttered. I can't do this.

Often, we get caught up making meditation one more thing that we have to do. It's so much more than completing a task. It's truly about showing up for yourself because that's all meditation is at the end of the day. The bottom line is you take the time to prioritize *yourself.*

How often do we even think about it like that? We usually think, oh, I have to find my answers. I have to talk to my higher self. I've gotta clear my mind. I've got to get ready for bed or try to get better sleep. We choose to meditate, but we're focused on putting expectations on the outcome rather than experiencing the feeling of the moment.

We give ourselves all these reasons to meditate, but what if we take the reasons away and make it about taking the time to lean in and listen? Ask yourself these questions before you start meditating:

- Do I get to gift myself a little self-care today?
- Can I show up for myself for just a few minutes today?

The more we start showing up for ourselves, the more we activate that honoring energy. When we activate that honoring energy, we really become more magnetic for the abundant lifestyle that we say we want anyways.

Because when we're honoring ourselves, we're really with our energy. We're opening our hearts and minds for the possibility of things that we want and kind of tying all those things together. It shifts the perspective instead of having one more thing that needs checking off the to-do list.

Instead of thinking of meditation as a chore, it's more about unwinding the task-driven nature of human beings. We're just moving into that quiet soul space to just show up for ourselves.

So how did I get from where I started to where I am now in my meditation practice? One tiny step at a time.

For me, it all started with a candle.

Lighting a candle and staring at the flame is a great first step on your journey to slowing your mind down. I think it feels almost hypnotic. You become entranced, and as you're watching that flame dance around, you sort of start noticing the energy around you softening because you become so laser-focused on that little flame.

It reminds me of sitting around a campfire with friends and family members. There comes a time when all the chatter dies down. No one is worried about interacting, and I'm not concerned with starting the next conversation. You're just there, right there. There's no need to entertain anyone.

I have time just to be me at that moment. And everyone else has time to quietly reflect on their inner thoughts. There's no room for comparison or drama. Everyone is at peace at that moment.

Keeping your eyes open and having something to look at is more manageable than closing your eyes when you're just starting to train yourself to be still. You are present with the candle's flame, and it's similar to romance movies when all the people blur away as the couple dances together. Except for this time, you're getting closer to tapping into your intuition and learning how to be with yourself on a deeper level.

I have had clients who said they laid down intending to keep their eyes closed, and after about a minute, they just couldn't do it anymore! The feeling of restlessness overpowered their good intentions. They had to open their eyes to check the time, their messages, their emails, and on and on. Their eyes jumped into phone withdrawal!

You could leave a lamp on, but that still kind of opens the door for potential distractions or overactivity of the mind. Don't have a candle handy? You can choose a spot on a wall. Try it for two minutes and set the timer on your phone so you don't get the urge to grab it and check the time.

Grab that journal. Write about a time when you "zoned out." Where were you? Was there something you were supposed to do at that time? How did you feel during and after that time? Beginning to meditate is that same kind of feeling. Are you ready? Sure, you are. Let's do this!

Try this:
- Light a candle or choose that spot on the wall.
- Go ahead and set your timer for two minutes.
- Just look at the flame or special spot on the wall. You don't need to think about anything else. You don't need to do anything with your body. You don't even need to worry about your breathing.

- Did the two minutes feel longer or shorter than you expected?
- How did you feel after the timer sounded at the two-minute mark?
- Were you fighting the urge to pick up your phone, or did you want to keep looking?

Write down anything that you noticed after your time was up. Set aside a few minutes each day and see if you can add a little more time each day. And before you know it, you've got your very own meditation practice! Just lean in and trust your instincts here, whether it's thirty more seconds or three more minutes. There are tons of guided meditation apps out there once you're comfortable with the concept of meditation.

Consider this:

Change cannot take place when you are stuck in the same old patterns, thoughts, and beliefs. You need a catalyst to help you move into a bigger and better life. It's all about honoring yourself and taking the time to sit with yourself in the present moment. Meditation is one way to feel that sense of relaxation and calm. Here are some others:

- Do things that make you laugh out loud. I love to watch comedies that make me experience those belly laughs that bring those joyful tears to my eyes.
- Interacting in nature. Go outside and put your bare feet in the grass. Take a walk at your local park or nature preserve. Keep your eyes open for birds, butterflies, or other little friends enjoying the day with you.

- Deep breathing. Slowing your breath slows your heart rate.
- Yoga is a great way to learn how to stay in the present moment and listen to your body.
- Find fun activities that activate your parasympathetic nervous system.

Don't overthink it. What matters the most is you're doing something! You are the vehicle that's going to transport yourself into that future version of yourself that you have your sights set on! The momentum is starting. Just keep moving forward!

My Reflections

You always have the power to choose
how you want to view the world
and your reality.

#LimitlessYou

You're Allowed to Choose Better.

*You cannot seek water from the one who drained your
seas, and you cannot build a home for your worth
inside another being. The medicine is when you return
to yourself, for you will remember your strength,
reclaim your own rhythm, write your new song.*
~ Victoria Erickson

N
ow you have a better understanding of self-care. You
have the first steps of your mediation practice. But you
may be thinking, "Okay. That's all well and good for this
lady with the Georgia-grown accent to tell me all these things,
but she has no idea what I've been through. I don't deserve my
partner beating on me. I didn't deserve to lose my home. I didn't
deserve all the abuse as a child. I didn't deserve losing everything to a robbery."

And to that, I say, you're right.

What you experienced was hurtful. So much was taken by the impact of the experience that sometimes you feel left with only the effect. And please hear me when I say what happened to you is not your fault.

If someone carried out an act that inflicted pain onto you, it doesn't mean that person gets to keep everything that you can ever be. You do not deserve to be their victim forever. You deserve to get back to being all that you are. You are allowed to feel your feelings when you consider this trauma. That anger, resentment, and rage are great tools that will lead you to change. To come back to your light and start feeling more like yourself again.

I want to get you out of the mind trap of your trauma. Time to walk away from the woulda, coulda, shoulda. This is the time to begin to forgive yourself for the circumstances surrounding the event. I will never tell you to sit in a circle and forgive those who wronged you. You're going to learn more about yourself and how to let go of so much of the angry and empty feelings and start learning more ways to get back to feeling whole and fulfilled as part of who you are. It is my wish to help you learn more about yourself, heal those old wounds, and move forward as the best version of yourself.

Maybe self-help has made you feel like you've brought horrible things into your life. So many thought leaders say things that lead you to believe you've created everything yourself. And it made you question, "Oh, so then I created this life with my abusive husband? Well great. I guess I'm just doomed to attract people who want to hurt me from now on."

Maybe you haven't had the experience of being able to have full validation of your feelings about your trauma. How many people have told you something like, *hey, it's been this many days/weeks/months/years, don't you think it's time to let it go and decide to move on?*

Please understand, these people love you and want to take your pain away. They simply don't know what to do to help you move forward in life. What they don't understand is the healing has to come from within *you*. My invitation here is for you to access more light, more possibilities, and more opportunities than you ever have before so that feeling can shine brighter for you than any of the darkness you've experienced up to this point in your life.

Think of yourself as an artist.

You're standing in front of a blank canvas. This is the canvas of your life. You have all the colors you'll ever need, and you're ready to create something beautiful. And so, it begins. You choose the first color and bring paint to canvas with that first brush stroke. There's a rush of excitement as you start to see your plan begin to take shape.

But then something shifts. You look over at the canvas belonging to the artist right beside you and start to compare your creation to theirs. A feeling of inadequacy washes over you. You hear a negative comment and let it become a part of your art. You limit the number of colors you allow yourself to choose. Then someone walks up and splashes paint right down the middle of your painting. What the heck? Why do we do this to ourselves?

Consider your mind. It has been tricked and trapped along the way. The tricks are the stories that you hear playing over and over. Things like, my painting isn't as good as hers. Or, he said it's ugly, so maybe I'm not an artist after all. We all have tricks like these floating around in our minds. They turn into traps when we start to believe that they're true. Then they solidify into non negotiables. Things like, she will always be better than me. I will never get his acceptance. I don't deserve to have a lot of paint to choose from on my personal palette. That's just how it is, and I need to stay here and accept that my life is just a small, unimportant existence and I should keep my head down and try to get through it.

Friend, this is where you're wrong. You don't have to believe the tricks, and you don't have to live within the framework of the traps. Today is the day to choose better. Sounds easy, right? If your answer is no, bear with me here.

Think about it. You make tons of choices every single day of your life.

Choices like what to wear, what to eat, who to call, what to listen to, what to read. You think these choices ultimately determine the trajectory of the day and your life because one leads to another, which leads to another, and so on.

But why is it that when it comes to choosing to honor yourself, you suddenly feel the need to hold back? Why can't you make choices that honor your inner feelings and your intuition when you know a choice is right? Is it to appease someone else? To ensure someone thinks better of you? Or because you feel like you must, so someone else's feelings don't get hurt?

Here you are, making choices day by day for every other reason than honoring your truest self. Then one day, you wake up and realize the weight of the world is on your shoulders and wonder how you ended up in this place. Does that sound familiar?

In life, you'll have these little moments of clarity that seem to creep up when they're most needed. Those moments belong to that little thing called your intuition. Over time, you can get pretty good at suppressing it or forgetting about it completely. It never seems to steer you wrong until you just ignore it or even choose the exact opposite of how you feel. Then your mind tricks activate, start scanning for stories to tell yourself, explaining why it was good not to listen, and your mind begins to look for every external circumstance to validate that story.

"Well, it's not safe for me to get into a new relationship because you can't trust people. See, Ken just cheated on Barbie last week!" Perfect validation, right?

Wrong.

Why limit yourself to one outcome of a situation based on another person's experience? You are perfectly and uniquely created, and you have an incredible journey called life to explore, design, and refine along the way.

So again, I ask you. Why do you want to predetermine what you can or can't have, change, or do because of someone else's story? When you do this, you allow the mind trap to solidify. You think you're playing it safe when in reality, you're stifling yourself. You're keeping your intuition buried, creating this illusion of what life is supposed to be that's based solely on societal rules and expectations, among other self-limiting beliefs.

The worst thing you can do to yourself is confine your soul into a predetermined box and never fully experience life. Not allowing yourself to change because change feels scary or too uncertain is such a small way to move through life. When you live in that space, you continuously tell yourself, "Oh, I can't do this because of that."

This was my life.

For years, I made choices from the trap of obligation, the fear of someone's negative opinion of me, the fear of my imperfections, and the trick that someone wanted me to make that choice. I lost sight of myself. I forgot who I was at my core. In my soul. At my most honest and pure level.

I never believed I could actually make choices for myself. I never realized that I could choose how I wanted my life to be, how I wanted to interact with others, and how I wanted to receive love and connection.

I thank God for the day this realization hit me. I woke up so lost and confused and heavy. I said, "Enough!" And I chose differently.

It's funny when you make an explicit declaration to God and the Universe like that, as you stand in your power and reignite who you were meant to be, even if it's just a little flicker, that flame will start to grow the more you lean into it. Things seem to line right up to open a new path for you that you never considered an option for your life before.

I had a hard time understanding that I had the freedom to choose at every moment. But once I got to that space, choice by choice, minute by minute, and day by day, I began to find myself again. I became reacquainted with the parts of me I thought other people and experiences wiped out long ago. But I was there all along, a little hidden, a little nervous, but there, waiting to be reclaimed once again.

It was the choices I made that put me there. How beautifully empowering to know this and to understand that my choices could dig deep and bring me fully back to life. I was willing. I was open. And I allowed change. I chose to change. I chose it over and over until every moment was more decadent. Each day was brighter and fuller of self-love and support, and encouragement from my biggest advocate (me!).

We live in a world of opposites.

Day and night. Light and dark. Happiness and sadness. Elation and despair. You get it. All these concepts are available to us all the time. And if all of it is available all the time, why would you want to trap yourself in the dark sadness for a lifetime? I want you to entertain this thought: what happens when you choose to move away from a limited life and into a *limitless* one? If we get to experience all of it, that means our active involvement needs to come forth so we can have it, be it, and do it.

So instead of saying, "I can't do this because of that," figure out how you *can*. By growing through the limiting belief, you can change everything. When you change your perspective, you allow yourself a new opportunity for growth. And when you do, you may just surprise yourself. You may achieve a new level of joy and happiness and fulfillment that you never thought was available to you before.

To be able to choose to move into a better situation, I need your active participation. I invite you to step outside your comfort zone today and choose one little thing you wouldn't usually choose. Make that first change. Allow your mind to release any limitations and just jump in. It can be big or small. Maybe you apply for the new job. Maybe you start by making a list of things you'd like to do, places you'd like to visit, or even a new food or recipe you'd like to try, but never took the time to follow up with that urge. Choosing differently, even in small doses, empowers you and sparks your inner light. It will shine brighter with each passing moment.

Let's activate a different part of your mind. Grab your journal and your pen. I'll wait.

I'd like to invite you to consider the following questions. You can think about them, write down your answers in words, or even draw them. This is a little shortcut to getting closer to the parts of you that have been hiding in the dark, if you're willing to try it out.

Going back to the idea of you as the painter of your life's canvas:

- What colors are you living through right now?
- What does your painting look like?
- What is the illustration of how you've carried yourself up until now?
- What would you prefer it to be?
- What would be better for you?
- How do you want to see it?

Try this:
- Make two fists.
- Tighten them as hard as you can.
- Feel into that compression.
- Consider what it would be like to relax them completely.
- In 3, 2, 1, let them go.
- What does it feel like to just let go?

Consider this:

- What is one area in your life right now that you are "white knuckling" your way through?
- What is that thing you're holding onto so tightly you can feel the tension the same way you felt it with that exercise?
- What is the worst thing you think would happen if you loosen that grip, even a little bit?
- What is the best thing that could happen if you let it go altogether?

Give yourself some time to look back over what you just put in your journal. Lean into how you feel as you do. Now, look at your hands wide open, with your palms facing up.

Remember, you need to have open hands in order to receive a gift. Right now, the gift you're moving toward is a deeper understanding of yourself. A chance to fully heal. A chance to be the most soul-aligned version of you.

And so, it begins.

If we can sort through our experiences,
mental chatter, and emotional clutter,
and then choose to shine at any moment,
why don't we?

#LimitlessYou

You're Allowed to Feel
Your Feelings.

Unexpressed emotions will never die. They are buried
alive and will come forth later in uglier ways.
~ Sigmund Freud

Growing up, my Nana was one of my favorite people on this earth. In her honor, please understand her name is pronounced "nawnaw." Not "naanuh." My Nana was the epitome of Southern hospitality and grace.

She was my world as I grew up. I loved being in the kitchen with her as she and my aunts were yackety-yacking around the kitchen, preparing for another gathering. You could hear the pots banging around, and there was just always so much activity. It makes me smile even now.

She was sharp as a tack, but at the same time, it was as though she was floating on a cloud. My brothers and I were spoiled rotten. I can still remember being amazed that this woman never raised her voice to us.

And when I started asking her about my dad's note he left behind, she'd turn to me with a faraway look in her eyes and say, "Oh Hunny, it's okay." And that was that. I knew the conversation was over. Not only did this woman lose an 8-month-old, but her beauty queen daughter also committed suicide when my dad was in college, and then he took his own life when I was in first grade. I never wanted to push her to talk about them because it felt disrespectful. But I couldn't understand why she seemed to keep all of her thoughts and feelings about them to herself.

I'm sure you've heard the term false positive, especially in 2020. But I want to look at this phrase from a different angle. So many people are living this way, and you may not even understand what you're doing.

Maybe you come home and realize that someone robbed your home. You start walking through the house, and everything's missing. The furniture's gone. Your clothes and jewelry are gone. All your kids' toys are gone. Everything. Is. Gone.

Except for the tv.

False positives are when you're not entirely truthful with yourself.

A false positive at this moment would be that you sit on the floor (where the couch used to be) with a smile plastered to your face as you grab the remote control and declare, "Well, at least they left the tv!"

You negate the truth of the fullness of the experience. Is that actually true to how you feel at the moment? Really?!

Maybe you say, "Someone broke into my freakin' house, and I'm so mad!"

Society tells us, "Mm mm mm (with a pointer finger wagging in your face), you'd better be *grateful* because it could have been so much *worse.*

You feel simultaneously torn. You feel so angry and unsafe and violated, and then you hear that little voice, "Uh uh uh. You do not get to express your true feelings fully. You just need to set that aside and start spouting off all the reasons you're happy about these circumstances, mmkay?"

What's happening is you're taking that negative experience and forcing yourself against your true feelings to turn it into something positive, and you make yourself find the silver lining.

And while there may be a part of you that is glad you still have a tv, and you're so relieved you weren't home when the people were taking your things, what are you really doing to yourself through the process of it?

You're literally telling yourself, "Nope. I do not honor you enough. I do not value you enough for these feelings and these emotions to come to the surface, to be expressed, and expelled." And you deprive yourself from the fullness of the experience.

So, if the fullness of the experience is that you needed to be angry, you needed to express rage, you needed to be in the space of disappointment, or distrust, or whatever the case may be, it's still there, floating around in your body. Waiting under the surface and begging to be heard.

Case study time!

A friend of mine grew up learning that her "bad" feelings weren't okay. She was an extremely sensitive kid living with traumatized and emotionally unavailable parents. Instead of understanding that her sensitivity was part of her, she often heard the phrase, "If you wanna cry, come here, and I'll give you something to cry about." That would scare her, so then she'd cry, and then she'd be hurt, and the cycle played out over and over until she moved in with other relatives. They also made fun of her for crying and teased her about being so weak. She was 12 years old.

As an adult, she decided to speak with a therapist. She was talking about a traumatic moment, and her therapist simply asked, "How did you feel at that moment?" But she couldn't answer the question. She'd say something like, "I thought…" and her therapist would gently ask again, "That's what you thought, but how did you *feel?"* It took an entire hour, a weighted blanket, a massive headache, and tons of tears for her to be able to express, "I felt *afraid.*"

What happened?

Remember those tricks and traps? As a child, her brain kept looking for evidence of the trick that having feelings brings physical pain. So over time, through the abuse she suffered, it solidified into the trap: I'm safer if I feel nothing. So, she lived most of her life in an emotionally neutral state——never too happy, never too sad, just right there in her perceived safe zone. Until the day she worked with a professional who helped her bring genuine feelings back into her reality.

That's an extreme example of stifling your feelings.

When faced with an emotion, we often make one of two choices: we stifle it or resist it. Our feelings get shoved down, or we replace them with something "more acceptable."

We label our feelings based on how others will look at us. We start thinking things like, "I can't express this emotion because they'll judge me. They'll see me as weak, helpless, frail, or a crybaby. It's just not acceptable for me to feel like this." Or we have this idea that if we face fear, doubt, sadness, or anger, and let ourselves feel those emotions, it will absolutely ruin us.

No one has taught us how to manage our feelings and emotions appropriately.

We're scared to death to deal with them. We feel like they're so much bigger than us that we must pretend they don't exist.

"Oh no, not me! I never get angry! Just look at my perfectly peachy outlook on life through my Facebook posts! Everything is under control, and I'm just naturally always this pleasant." That, my friends, is the attitude of someone clinging to the false positive.

And then this person is at the grocery store, and someone cuts the line. Oh, it's on! She's immediately furious. She's making loud angry comments about the line-jumper to the poor person behind her, looking for an ally who agrees with her that she was *wronged and disrespected*. But deep down, it has nothing to do with the line-jumper and everything to do with the feeling that she is constantly letting other people set her feelings aside and disrespect her boundaries, and it just blows up.

Have you ever found yourself in a perfectly pleasant conversation with someone, and then suddenly, you are agitated and extremely put off by something they've said? Like the rage just poured out of you. Then you get home and have a minute to settle down, and you don't even remember why you were mad at them?

Or, months after the robbery, you're sitting on your new couch watching the tv you were "so grateful" they left behind. Something pops up that vaguely feels like your experience, or you see a news story and get all fired up and start yelling, "See! These people always get away with blah blah blah."

That's precisely what happens when you choose to suppress instead of expressing your feelings.

That false positive pushed those "bad" feelings down, but they don't just go away. You planted those little seeds, and they fester and grow deep down. And they keep popping up over and over until you make the conscious choice to sit with them, genuinely hear them, and then let them go.

"Okay, Holly, that's all well and good, but you don't know anything about my experience. You don't understand all the awful experiences I've had to wade through. I'm ready to throw this dang book across the room right now and never pick it up again!"

Is that you? Are you feeling triggered just by reading about false positives? Good. That's actually a step in the right direction.

Because guess what? Those buried feelings are burning and bubbling within you at this very moment. It's time for you to face them. And then you can release them out of your heart. That's the beauty of it! Once you let yourself feel them, you can release them, and they won't be with you anymore.

As a society, we need to finally walk away from the shame culture that says we need to be in a state of perpetual gratitude. If it isn't a genuine feeling, it will do far more harm than good. You can end up with physical ailments when you keep bottling up your feelings hour after hour, day after day, and year after year! Please hear me when I say you're worth so much more than that!

My question to you is simple.

How do you really feel? Angry? Sad? Misunderstood? Alone?

Whatever it is, sit with the feeling.

Now I'm not saying go out and avenge yourself for all the wrongdoings in this world. I'm asking you to give yourself the space to recreate the narrative that put those feelings in your heart and kept them there. What happened? What were the circumstances that brought you to suppressing instead of expressing your feelings back then?

As you consider the event, go ahead and allow yourself to say it out loud, "I feel (fill in the blank)." It's not something you need to call someone else to express. This is a moment for you to sit with yourself, lean in, really listen, and then dig that out of your heart. This is the moment when you permit yourself to go there. Why do you have that emotion attached to that event?

Grab your journal! It's time to dig deep. Think of your brain as a highway. There are lanes and off-ramps everywhere. In a perfect situation, all the feet are on the gas pedals. Every car is going with the flow, and everyone is getting to where they want to go with ease.

But when you are holding your feelings back, brake lights are popping up here and there. Traffic is lurching in other spots, and in some places, the cars sit still with no knowledge of what's going on or when they can get moving again, if ever.

- What are your avenues for expression?
- Where are the biggest traffic jams on your highway?
- What is causing them?
- Are there some off-ramps you need to take for a moment of rest?
- How can you clear up the traffic to get those cars flowing along with ease?

Try this:
- Find a quiet place to go with your notebook and pen.
- Close your eyes and take three big breaths in and out. Inhale for three seconds, hold it for three seconds, and then exhale for three seconds.
- Keeping your eyes closed, ask yourself, "What feelings do I need to deal with? Where are they coming from?"
- Stay in that stillness and just listen to yourself. When you get an answer, don't hesitate.
- Permit yourself to just write without thinking. Just get it all onto the paper.

· Then once it's all out, read it back slowly. It's okay to feel emotional as you read it back. Whatever you feel—sadness, anger, grief—is true to you. There is no need to attach guilt or shame here.

Consider this:

· What is the best thing that could happen if you express yourself openly and honestly?
· How do you talk to yourself about your feelings? Is that self-talk yours, or did your brain pick up a trick over time?
· How would your life be different if you honored your feelings all the time?

Take the time to look back over what you've just written. Did anything pop up on paper that surprised you? Try not to add any judgment to those feelings. Decide the best way to express them and take action.

Maybe you need to go for a run. Perhaps you need to take a drive and sing your favorite songs at the top of your lungs to get it out (and you may make someone else's day as they see you). It might be time to go into your room and punch the crap out of your pillow. Or just throw an old-fashioned temper tantrum in the middle of your living room, complete with tears and stomping feet.

I know it can be painful at the moment when you bring up those old scenes, but once you recognize those feelings and let them be heard and released, it will make a massive difference in your overall well-being. Whatever you need to do to get that release is suitable for you. Make sure you drink a lot of water and if you feel drained, honor yourself for putting in the work and take some time to rest.

Give yourself some grace. You just released feelings that you buried a long time ago. That's a huge step toward healing old wounds and moving closer to the person you've been all along.

Well done!

My Reflections

Before you get out of bed in the morning,
think of something that makes you smile.
If you do this every day, you have no choice
but to raise your vibes!

#LimitlessYou

Reevaluate Your Thoughts.

We are what our thoughts have made us;
so take care about what you think.
Words are secondary.
Thoughts live; they travel far.
~Swami Vivekananda

I remember going to a job interview shortly after completing my Psychology degree. There I was, fresh out of college and ready to enter the workforce. The interview felt like it was going well. I mean, it *was* going well until the interviewer said, "Tell me a little about yourself." And at that moment, I decided I didn't know *anything* about myself! I knew about psychology, and all the reasons I was qualified for the job. But what could I say about *myself?* I remember being so frozen at that moment.

I was utterly dumbfounded. I sat there wracking my brain, filled with all this frantic energy. My thoughts were swirling around like a tornado as I tried reaching for anything and everything I could possibly grab onto, but there was no use. I could not formulate and express anything coherent at that moment. I said the first thing that felt like a sentence.

I'm sorry to say that the best I came up with was, "I like cats?" And yes, it was more like a question as I shrugged my shoulders and held my hands up in a surrender pose.

What the heck, Holly?! I knew that wasn't an appropriate answer. And what began as a standard interview question turned into an existential crisis that ended in me not knowing anything about who I was other than my preference for animals!

It all comes back to what happened to my brain over time. As I grew up, I solidified the trap that I couldn't trust my thoughts. I took the role of a people-pleaser. In relationships with boyfriends, I chose to let them think for me. If I said I wanted a burger, and he said, "Nah, let's get some pizza!" I decided pizza sounded better anyway.

Or if we'd get ready to go out, I'd check in with him on my outfit choice. Suppose I got a nod of approval, awesome. But if not, it was back to the closet to get something that would make me think he was happy with my choice.

See that subtle difference? I never felt like it was a big deal. Most times, I would chalk it up to changing my mind instead of giving away my power and letting other people change my mind for me. Something you do about a million times shows your brain an easy, predictable, and safe pattern. And I'd remind myself that having his choice tasted just fine, or the first outfit wasn't really what I wanted to wear. It didn't matter anyway.

Except it did. And over time, I spiraled deeper and deeper, losing myself more and more until I was in the middle of an abusive relationship, sitting on the floor with my eyes closed, wondering if my next breath would be my last. When I realized how close to dying I had come, I knew I had to take charge and put myself first.

Now I'm not saying that deferring a decision here and there in an attempt to please other people will turn into not knowing who you are in a job interview. And I'm not saying it will take a traumatic event to push you into thinking for yourself again. But I *am* saying it's time to take a dive into your thoughts and see whose they are and whose they are not.

Your thoughts are extremely powerful.

And they most certainly shape the way you see and interact with the world around you. Understanding your thoughts and letting go of some that don't serve you will help change how you live your life.

Let's say you want to live a happier life. You even say it out loud, "I want to be happier!" But at the same time, there is a place in the back of your mind whispering, nope, I don't deserve to be happy. Or maybe you're thinking, nothing good happens to me, so saying I want to be happy won't make a difference anyway.

Or maybe you're in a meeting for work. And there is that one coworker, sitting in the front row, all smiles and full of ideas. You don't know why, but her presence irritates you to no end. You roll your eyes and wish she'd just move to the back of the room and be quiet for once.

But let's get real here for a second. Weren't you just thinking that you have great ideas too? Didn't you just tell your friend that you want to be more involved in meetings? So why is the person who does what you'd like to do tend to drive you crazy at meetings? Humor me for a second here.

Could it be true that when you find people annoying or frustrating, they're a reflection of who *you* want to be? And could it be that you find yourself objecting to that person because you see a part of who you won't let yourself become in who they are? In this instance, who are you really frustrated with—the person who isn't afraid to openly share ideas, or yourself?

Do you see what you're doing?

You're giving your brain mixed signals. You say you want to be happy and contribute to meetings at work. But then, when the opportunity shows itself, the negative and limiting thoughts show up louder than the positive whispers of what you really want. You tell yourself that you aren't worthy of sharing your ideas, and that thought doesn't really align to who you are, so you're frustrated with someone else who isn't experiencing that same kind of internal conflict.

Those mind traps are so negative and solid sometimes that even if we don't want them in our lives anymore, they keep showing up again and again. And the sad part is we have this idea that if a thought shows up in our brains, it has to be the truth. Plain and simple.

Our brains contain lots of old stories filled with limits. We don't need them if we're going to grow. And most of the time, those limits didn't even come from us in the first place! But sometimes, our brains are just telling us what it thinks we want to hear.

So how do we change this pattern? It's time to start trusting yourself again, my friend. But how can you make conscious choices to trust yourself and your thoughts?

It won't happen overnight, and you won't be able to just sit on the couch and say you're going to trust yourself from that moment forward. You have to take the time to become more consciously aware of your thoughts and where they are coming from in order to get clear on what you want out of life. That way, you can start to let go of the thoughts that no longer serve you.

It's time to choose to lean in and be aware. You can choose to learn. You can choose to embrace this new knowledge. It all sounds great, right? But how will you implement it, so you end up with the life you deserve?

Some people fall into the trap and think, "If I treat myself well, I must be pretty darn selfish." Or they go in a different direction as they embrace self-sacrifice and think, "My feelings don't matter, and as long as everything outside of me is working, I don't need to feel amazing on the inside."

The main question you need to ask yourself is, "Does this choice add value, honor, and dignity to myself and others?"

Start to observe your behaviors and actions.

When you choose to honor yourself, you feel it in your guts and your emotions. Think about a time in your childhood when you were proud of yourself. Did you smile from ear to ear? Did you jump up and down? Did you have some happy tears running down your face?

We are constantly making choices. On the one hand, you reinforce the trust you have for yourself. And on the other, you are strengthening your sense of need, control, distrust, or disempowerment, and you start to embrace thoughts like, "I give up. I don't wanna do this."

When you don't trust yourself, you're like this scared little turtle. You wander through life thinking, "Let me hide in my little shell. I need to protect myself at all times. Everything's unsafe, everything is uncertain, and everything's just overwhelming and scary!"

But when you trust yourself, the narrative changes completely. You strut around thinking, "I'm empowered, I am strong, and I can handle it all, no matter what! Bring it on!"

Take some time to think about the two circumstances below. Write them down in your journal for a time of reflection later.

- When have you felt the most alive? Think about a moment when everything happened with great ease and flow. What happened? Did your reaction remind you of that childlike joy? What did it feel like? What emotions were present? What was your internal chatter? In what ways did you feel validated by the experience, on the inside or the outside? Were you on fire and ready to put your head down and get to work?
- Think about a complex experience or decision you faced. Did you feel shaky or sweaty about the choice? Did you

suddenly feel like you couldn't catch your breath? You may have thought something along the lines of, "Oh my gosh, I just can't do this." What did you do? Did you look outside of yourself to make the decision? Did you avoid making a choice? Did the feeling cause you to shut down altogether?

Most of us teeter between these two kinds of circumstances. One is a life with trust, and the other is a life of distrust. Understand, you have a choice in how you want to live your life.

Think of your brain as a golden retriever.

Stay with me here. Golden retrievers are known for being excellent at going and getting things and bringing them back to you, right? What you think about is what your brain will show you. It's a wild game of subconscious fetch that everyone plays from time to time.

Not too long ago, my husband was looking for a particular kind of truck. We were talking about it and going around to different dealerships looking for one. Then as I started driving around running errands, it started feeling like they were all over the dang place! And wouldn't you know it, I turned a corner, and there it was! We saw the exact truck he wanted, right there on the corner of a dealership's lot.

Did this ever happen to you? If you ever thought about having a child, did you suddenly see pregnant people everywhere? Or when you looked for your first home, were there houses for sale at every turn? This can happen with things we want just as much as with things we don't want but think about all the time. And that is when we can get tricked into thinking it has to be true if we keep seeing the same negative things, circumstances, or behaviors from others.

- What do you consistently ask your brain to fetch?
- Do you see more positive things or negative things coming to you?
- What is causing these thoughts?
- Are they your thoughts, or do they belong to a person or an old experience?
- Are you ready to make a change (if you're reading this, that answer is *yes!*)?
- What can you start to look for that will help you trust yourself again?

Time for your active participation!

Try this:

Let me give you some action steps to get your trust back. The more you reinforce self-trust, the easier it will come to you.

- Start to take responsibility for yourself, emotions, and behavior. Give yourself permission to experience the fullness of each moment, recognize them, and move forward.
- Choose to take care of your well-being on all levels. Notice how you talk to yourself and start being nice! Be your biggest cheerleader! Choose to honor your body without getting angry or fighting yourself over something like eating a piece of cake. You

can decide you are enjoying the cake from a place of valuing the experience instead of coming from an angry place saying something like, "I'm eating this stupid piece of cake because I don't care about that dang diet. It isn't working anyways."

·   Be aware of the little tricks that try to tell you that no one can be trusted, including yourself. Right now, think of three things that happened when you trusted yourself, and it was a fantastic experience.

·   Let go of thinking that you must be in control of every situation. When you work on trusting yourself from within, you automatically begin to release the idea that you have to control and manipulate every situation.

Consider this:

·   What is the best thing that could happen if you choose to trust yourself?

·   How do you talk to yourself? Can you change what you say (hint: *Yep!*)?

·   How would your life be different if you chose to believe in yourself every minute of every day?

We need to get to the point where we don't have to run ourselves through the filters of what other people may think. It's time to start finding validation from within. And if someone agrees, cool! But if they disagree, you need to understand that disagreement does not mean you need to change who you are to live harmoniously with them.

If you tremble at the thought of an interviewer saying, "Tell me a little about yourself," don't panic! Start by really listening to what you say to yourself and how much you trust those thoughts. You can start with those small steps. And before you know it, those feelings of self-empowerment and trust will be automatic.

My Reflections

Today you are free from the illusion
that tries to keep you afraid.

#LimitlessYou

Let Go of Your Victimhood and Surrender.

Growth demands a temporary surrender of security.
~ Gail Sheehy

I lost my dad when I was in first grade.

I was on my bedroom floor playing Barbies with my friend when the door burst open. Her mom scooped her up and left, and I watched the chaos that was my family. There had been an accident with a gun. My dad was gone. So much was happening it was almost like I left my body as my family members stood in a line there, each feeling the gravity of the moment in their own way. As I think about that moment even now, it's still like I was just an observer. I don't remember feeling any profound emotions.

My six-year-old brain created a story around my dad's death. I told myself that he must have had a shotgun in the backseat that went off by accident when he hit a bump going over the railroad tracks. I can still see him dancing around the house and being silly. My last memory of him was playing a game of Monopoly. For some reason, we didn't finish it because he got up and left in the middle of the game. I don't know where he was going or what made him feel like he needed to leave the game without finishing it with us.

It wasn't until I turned fourteen that my Aunt Harriet told me that he had taken his life.

And he left a note behind. That was a huge shock to my system, to say the least.

I felt so betrayed and hurt. Why didn't my family tell me the truth sooner? Why tell me at all if they kept it from me for so many years? What happened to the note? What did it say? Did he say anything directly to me? Where in the world was it now? Did someone throw it away? I remember tearing through Nana's house, trying to find it. Rage and anger buzzed throughout my body, and I could hardly think straight. Could I trust the family that I loved so much? If they lied to me about my dad, what else were they lying about?

The hurt was so profound. I decided as a teenager to lock myself in a kind of emotional cage. I never wanted to feel so hurt ever again. I decided I'd create my own kind of superpower. If I didn't feel anything, no one could hurt me, nothing would surprise me, and I'd be tough. I surrounded myself with emotionally unavailable people and it worked. Until it didn't.

I got married at the ripe old age of 19.

He was addicted to heroin, and I was in denial. I was doing laundry, and when I was pulling the laundry basket from the shelf, a syringe and spoon fell to the floor. I called my friend and started chewing her out about doing drugs in my house. Her response was, "Holly, you need to take a look at what's right in front of you." I still didn't want to believe her.

A few nights later, I woke up gasping for air. I couldn't get my husband to wake up and help me, so I ran to the hospital myself. My uvula had swollen due to some kind of allergic reaction, and I couldn't speak. The doctors couldn't figure out why it happened, but they could help the swelling. After it settled down and I could breathe safely again, I walked home.

As I got closer to the driveway, something told me to look in the car. I lifted the floor mat and found what could have been a Drugs Are Us superstore. There was no way I could deny what was happening any longer. I went into the house to confront my husband. He was still asleep when I lifted the sheets and saw the marks on his arms. I knew it was time to get divorced. But when we separated, I felt overrun with guilt. I kept thinking; how could I leave someone who needed me to fix him?

Deciding that I needed a fresh start, I moved to Atlanta, still broken from that relationship. I got married again and was pregnant within months. He was a narcissist, and I was in denial. He became physically abusive. We moved back home and were living in the same house across from Nana's. My daughter was five weeks old when it all unraveled.

He pushed me, and my tooth chipped as my head hit the doorframe. And when he kicked open the bedroom door, something finally clicked in my mind. My baby was lying in the bassinet, and I knew I wasn't going to live like that anymore.

I heard a little voice inside say, *"You must survive. This is all you've got."*

The pain I felt moments before was replaced with some serious mama bear instincts. Some kind of mix of adrenaline and self-preservation gave me the strength to shove that man away from the bedroom, through the living room, and out the front door. That divorce was volatile, of course. I gave up everything he wanted, and I became a single mom.

So why are these stories in the chapter about victimhood? I need you to see that I could have chosen to live there for the rest of my life, but I didn't. And you don't have to either.

I'm a survivor of domestic abuse. When I finally got out of it and looked back, the thought crossed my mind, *I must be some special kind of idiot to take this for so long!* When you're in the middle of a situation like that, it's so easy to make excuses and believe the lies that your life no longer belongs to you or that you're incapable of making big decisions.

So, how did I get to that day when I woke up and realized I deserved better? How did I decide to remove myself from the relationship?

Surrender.

When I say surrender, I don't want you to think of me waving a white flag in the air and admitting defeat. That's not what I mean. This kind of surrender is a positive action. Not surrendering to the abuse. Not succumbing to the pain. But letting go of the fear, guilt, and shame that kept me there and surrendering to the possibility of a better life.

I needed to admit that I had shut off the part of me that saw my value. I did not deserve a relationship like that. As a matter of fact, no one does. When I thought about my baby and the life we were living, I knew I had to change the direction of our lives, or we weren't going to make it.

Your first step to leaving a life of victimhood is the ability to believe that something different needs to happen and that it *is* possible to take responsibility for that change.

In order to understand how to surrender, you need to understand what it means to live a life filled with blame.

It's so easy to give our power away. And if we spend most of our time blaming others for our circumstances, it actually creates the mind trick that we are safe.

Now stay with me here.

If everything is happening *to* us, we can't take any responsibility for what's irritating or upsetting us. And with that feeling of lack of control, we don't need to find solutions to the deeper root cause of the issues. When we blame others, it can release us from the uncomfortable feelings that need to be felt, healed, and released.

If I could blame the drugs for the problems in my first marriage, I wouldn't have to ask myself why I decided to marry him in the first place. I could justify staying with him by blaming the drugs and saying that he needed me to stay so I could fix him and make him better. But the truth is, you can't help someone who doesn't think they need help in the first place. It didn't matter how much I wanted him to live a happy and healthy life, his choices were his own, and unless he genuinely wanted to change, I was powerless.

I could have said that I was cursed by the time I was in the middle of my second marriage and just decided, welp, this is the best I can do. I could come at it from fear and lack and think that I had to just be careful and cautious and live with the abuse because I needed to stay married to be able to make it financially. Deep down, I knew that I was worthy of love and connection with a man who treated me well. And there was no way I wanted my sweet baby girl to grow up in an environment of fear like that. There was no other choice but to end that marriage as a way to honor her and myself.

When I began to surrender to the idea that I could have a say in how I lived my life, things began to change for the better. Let me show you how surrender saved me and led me into a much better life filled with beautiful synchronicities.

There I was. A newly single mama with a baby girl to support.

I became a night janitor at a daycare for my second job. If you've never had the pleasure of working a job that involves cleaning a bathroom after little children have been using it all day, count yourself blessed! I don't know what possessed children to write on bathroom stalls with their own poop, but I spent many nights scrubbing away at their artwork, reminding myself that this was only the beginning of a new life for us.

That janitor position came from a friend whose parents owned the school. When she offered the job to me, I remember saying, "I'll take it. I don't care." I knew it wouldn't be a permanent position, but it was steady money at the time.

Now we've already discussed false positives, and you can bet I had to face my ego and work through my feelings of despair and embarrassment when I noticed a group of women making their way into the auditorium. One had a speaker system, and they were all in color-coordinated workout clothes, chatting away as they entered and got set up. Then the music started playing, and I realized what was happening.

I froze. There I was with a bucket and mop going around this private school and daycare, and here are these wealthy women coming into the school for an after-hours jazzercise class for fun (and in my mind), without a care in the world! I thought I could just wait them out and clean after they'd gone home for the night. But wouldn't you know it? There were two classes that the lady was leading. I couldn't wait it out, so I had to swallow my pride, get in there, and do what I needed to do. It was time to clean the building.

Living in a small Southern town, pretty much everybody knows everyone else *and* all of their business. Between those two jazzercise classes, I just knew there would be someone who would recognize me. I remember thinking, *"Someone just drown me in this toilet right now. I can't face this!"*

I had to surrender to the idea that this job would lead to something better even though the evidence wasn't there yet. I could have thrown a temper tantrum, threw down my mop, and said, *"Forget this. I'm out of here."* But I worked around those exercisers, scrubbed the poop paintings, and reminded myself that this was a first step in the right direction for me and my baby. You just never know what's lurking around the corner when you can stay in a place of trust.

After several months, the same friend who helped me get the janitor's job suggested that I apply to a job at a company where she was working. She had heard of the opening, and I was the first person who came to mind. She said, "You're such a go-getter. I know you can do this job. Will you please just apply?'

I could have easily decided not to apply.

I could have stayed in victim mode and thought, "Why would a company hire someone who is cleaning a school at night for their open position?" But that wasn't the case.

I remember thinking, I'm just doing this right now. It isn't who I am. They don't know all of my past mistakes. They can't judge me. That was a huge one for me! I felt humiliated and like a failure in life after going through two divorces, and I wanted to hide from any type of judgment.

I sat down to get my resume together, and this feeling washed over me. *Heck yeah! I'm capable.* My friend looked it over, put it on the pile, and reminded me to put her down as a referral. In less than twenty-four hours, I had an interview scheduled! *I may need to learn some specifics, but I am absolutely capable of doing this.*

I had three different jobs at that time while family members babysat for me. By day I worked in insurance. I had my janitorial duties at night. And on the weekends, I went to stores as a pet food representative. Getting this new job would allow me to pare down.

On the day that I had my interview, a man named Danny went to the office for his own interview, taking a drive from his home in Alabama to Georgia. We missed each other by an hour. This is important later, trust me.

I ended up with an interview and was offered the job within days of applying. I checked in with my employers about giving them notice and stayed on with the weekend job for a while. I had resolved to keep my head down and work hard to raise my daughter without worrying about starting a new relationship. But the universe had a different plan.

At the new job, I experienced rapid growth.

I kept moving to the next level and then the next. I ended up with my own office and was working with sales consultants who sold heating and air. Danny would call asking for parts that we needed to ship to customers, and we developed a great long-distance working relationship. One day, he and a co-worker came to Georgia for something. I don't remember what he needed that day, but I certainly won't forget meeting him face to face for the first time. I walked out of my office, and he was there in the hall.

I went right up to him and said, "Oh my gosh, you're Danny!" And I *hugged* my co-worker. He wasn't quite sure why I was hugging him. Honestly, I didn't know either! But we got a good laugh out of it. We continued to grow our working relationship after that meeting, neither of us looking for anything more.

A job opened up in Alabama. I just knew it would be good for me to make a move. But I wasn't sure that I could just up and sell my house. But get this: one day, a lady down the street knocked on my door. I could see the moving trucks in front of her house. She was trying to fight back the tears as she informed me that she and her kids got evicted from their home. She didn't want her kids to have to leave their school, and she didn't know what to do.

Without a second thought, I asked her if she wanted to rent my house. She couldn't believe it, and frankly, I couldn't either. But it made perfect sense! So just like that, I couldn't say that I had to stay in Georgia because I needed to stay in my house that I didn't want to sell. That fast, I had a way to cover my mortgage payments. We made a little contract right then and there with a pen and a paper towel, and our neighbors helped her move in as I moved out!

Some guilt crept in as I prepared to move to Alabama. I had just lost my brother, Aunt Harriet, and Bill (did you ever call your grandpa by his first name? We did!). I worried about leaving Nana on her own. But instead of canceling my plans altogether, I made it work. I decided I'd spend weekends with her and drive from Georgia to Alabama on Mondays to start my work week. I'm grateful for the time we got to spend together on those weekends.

In Alabama, Danny and I continued to work together. He was the general manager, and I was the sales coordinator. We talked every day, because we worked together, but also because we were developing a friendship. Humor and silly conversations between us deepened our bond. And we grew together as friends without expectations of anything more because we were both dealing with past hurts.

Surrender played a part in the way my life changed for the better.

I could have told myself to stay in an abusive marriage just to keep from having to work three jobs to support my daughter. I could have chosen not to apply for a new job when my friend told me I should. I could have decided to stay in Georgia in the house I just bought. I could have said that taking a job in a different state was selfish and that I should stay and take care of Nana full time instead. But all those moments of surrender led me to meet my best friend, who I am now so very honored to call my husband.

Sometimes we get tricked into thinking it's easier to stay in a miserable situation instead of moving into an unknown future. And although there is some element of comfort in the familiar, there are times when leaving the comfortable behind and surrendering to the idea of a better future is the right choice.

It's like using a flashlight on a dark night. You can only see as far as the beam of light, but you trust that as you move forward, it will continue to illuminate more of the path you're on, so you keep taking one step at a time without fear of what's just beyond what you can see.

I'd like to invite you to consider the following questions. You can think about them, write down your answers in words, or even draw them. Just make sure you actively participate with these questions in some way to let the answers stay with you.

Where are you leaning on victimhood to keep you in a seemingly safe place?

- What is taking the blame for you staying put?
- When you think about making a change, what reasons or excuses keep popping up?
- Where are those reasons coming from?
- Do they feel like a safe, predictable pattern?

Try this:

It's time to think about mastering the art of living a limitless life. Try these strategies to disarm the victim mentality and embrace your power.

- Recognize the mental drain. Start noticing when you feel isolated and in pain, then lean in for yourself and intentionally look for positive factors in your life. Make a choice to move towards healing that sadness or pain with a small first step.
- Avoid seeking out a rescuer. Remind yourself that you have the power within you to make meaningful changes in your life without having to wait for someone else to swoop in and save you.
- Meditate. Meditation helps you to be able to take a step back from the situation and be an observer. It can help you become more self-aware and help you to cope with negativity and stress in a new way.

Consider this:

- Life might be challenging right now, but you always have a choice.
- What is one small step you can take that will move you forward?
- What is the worst thing that could happen if you made a change?
- What is the best thing that could happen if you made a change?

Beyond the shadow of a doubt, I can tell you that my life is entirely different than it was only a few years ago. When you can surrender to the idea of a better future, you connect more closely with your soul. And when you align with your soul, your life starts to evolve in ways that feel like little miracles surround you and move you closer to the life you deserve.

Understanding who you are and
what has been keeping you from being
the fullest expression of your infinite being
is the place where you gain the courage
to live a limitless life!

#LimitlessYou

Set Up Your Power Pedestal.

Be true to yourself, stay focused and stay you, take advice from other folks, use what you can, but never mind what is not for you. For the most part, trust yourself and believe in what you are doing.

~ Musiq Soulchild

Up to this point, you've uncovered so many pieces of yourself that came to you through conditioning or other variations of attaching to or allowing other people's opinions and belief systems to tangle up with your own, and I'm so proud of you! Now it's time to embrace who you are and where you stand on your own. Who are you at your core, without looking through the filters you used to take on from society, friends, and family members, or those tricks and traps you chose to leave behind?

When you can understand the most authentic version of yourself, you get to embrace unconditional self-love. And when you get to that point, so many limitations that you held onto start to fade away because they weren't even yours from the beginning. It's truly an amazing feeling when you can let all of it go and stand firmly in who you are at your core.

Now, it's time to create and begin to cultivate your power pedestal. Your pedestal is the foundation upon which you stand. It holds your vision and mission for your life, along with your beliefs. It answers all the questions:

- Who are you at a soul level?
- How do you want to claim your authenticity?
- How do you want to demonstrate your truth?
- How do you want to be the most authentic version of yourself?

When you create your power pedestal, guilt and shame don't belong here anymore! Guilt is when you make a poor choice or a wrong decision that goes against your integrity. But shame eats at your soul because it makes you feel inadequate, unworthy, and unlovable at your core. This is when you can feel fearful of exploring your untapped potential. The best part? You can finally answer those questions without turning to anyone but yourself, without activating all those old patterns and belief systems you picked up along the way.

It's essential to believe that change is possible when you align to your truth. Many of those old emotions will start to pop up when you choose big, amazing things for yourself. I'm not going to lie—change is disruptive! Your brain jumps into fight, flight, faint or freeze, right? It'll get in your head and shake up whatever used to feel comfortable and safe. Patterns start to show up, and your new ability to lean in and see them as no longer applicable to you is what makes all the difference as you grow into the truest version of *you*.

Your truth has changed, so now it's time to change the narrative and let your power pedestal guide you. Your behaviors, mindset, and patterns will look different from here on out. They are so much more in alignment with the real you! And yes, that's a good thing.

When you bolster the innate, wholesome qualities that you value about yourself, you begin to strengthen your energy and yourself. When you live in this space, you no longer become influenced by anyone or any circumstance outside of yourself. You'll surprise yourself when those old fears just stop showing up after really diving in and practicing the steps in this chapter.

Time for a case study!

A friend of mine struggled with hypervigilance due to PTSD. She was always on the lookout for grave danger, and it was a scary and exhausting way to live as her brain accepted the challenge and gave her horrible stories of all the bad things that could happen. But after years of therapy, she was on vacation with her family. She and her husband took their teenage boys ziplining. They had a great day together on the guided tour through the treetops. As they walked out to the parking lot, she suddenly realized that there wasn't one moment when she thought about one of her family members plunging to an untimely death. It was definitely a day to celebrate all of the work she put in to change her thought patterns because fear was not a part of her truth anymore.

The stronger you become with knowing, understanding, and living your truth, the harder it is to let those influences into your mind, physical body, heart, and soul. You're strengthening your sense of personal empowerment here. And that's what makes it so fun! You're expanding and embracing your power!

Even when you have moments of feeling unsure of what to do or say, you'll find that because you did the work and know exactly who you are and what you believe in, you can understand how to support yourself throughout the process.

Any time you feel hopeless or ineffectual, you also feel disempowered. But, when you fuel yourself with empowered energy, you can become limitless and access all of that untapped potential within! Developing your power pedestal helps restore your autonomy and engage in empowerment in all of your choices and interactions.

When you start to work with your untapped potential, that's when you notice that you're acting within that flow state. It feels like information is extremely easy to access. Things just come to you without even having to ask for them. Ideas are pouring into your mind, solutions to problems feel effortless. Creative sparks are all over the place, and the energy is almost palpable. You don't have to question anything from a flow state. But if you do ask a question, the answer automatically shows up!

Empowerment breeds self-love and acceptance. It is the epitome of belief, hope, and support. So, when you start to notice that you begin to reject yourself in any way, I want you to ask, "Do I feel empowered right now?" And if the answer is no, you are in a moment that needs to be challenged, acknowledged, and healed.

Let's get to it!

Your first step is to understand the greatness that you hold inside of yourself. It's time to grab your journal and tap in for personal reflection. By putting your thoughts in writing, you allow them to solidify as your truth.

Consider a challenge you lived through. Rather than seeing the pain of the trauma, it's time to find your power within that situation. This is not a way to diminish your trauma by any means. But to create that sense of balance and bring you back to your wholesome qualities, it's imperative to understand that the challenge or trauma you faced wasn't the end for you. You put yourself back together, maybe not in a way that aligns with your ultimate truth, but this is the time to merge some of your survival tendencies with your truth.

Write your answers to these questions:

- What skills did you develop?
- What information did you learn?
- In what area did you grow?
- How were your strength, courage, and confidence catalyzed?
- How did you demonstrate self-care?
- What is the gift that came from the challenge?

Now it's time to consider a time of celebration in your life. Consider a high point in your life's story. Answer these questions next:

- What is one incredible success you experienced?
- What endowments do you cherish the most in your life?
- Describe your most empowered memory. What qualities or characteristics of greatness stand out the most for you?

In psychology, it's a common practice to identify what you believe. If you don't align to your truth, it's easy to let the beliefs and values of those people outside of you dictate your life's path! To know where you want to go in life, you must understand who you are at this core level.

And guess what? When you have your power pedestal nailed down, those beliefs allow you to:

- Realize that you're already enough.
- Believe in yourself and your capabilities.
- See life as an opportunity to grow rather than a struggle to get through.
- Confidently make decisions based on love rather than fear.
- Live according to your values and integrity.
- Source your sense of power and self-worth from within.
- Prioritize self-expression and your soul's mission over the fears of judgment and rejection.
- Highlight your intuition and gut feelings rather than logical and analytical thinking.
- Experience your thoughts, feelings, and beliefs as temporary and changeable instead of a concrete identity.

As you develop it, keep in mind the energy, emotions, and experiences that pop up as you consider each category. Those doubts, fears, and insecurities will show up. But they aren't there to tell you to go back to living a small life. They're letting you know that it's time to get ready for something big that's on its way! Now that you took the time to glimpse your greatness, use those feelings to develop your new power pedestal.

Alright, grab that journal again. It's time to explore your standards and values and make some changes. For each of the categories below, do a little brain dump. Write down anything that comes to mind about them, and then you can decide where they originated. For now, though, just jot it all down. There are no stupid responses, just write!

Ready? Here you go! What are your immediate thoughts regarding:

- Character values?
- Work values?
- Personal values?
- Family values?
- Spiritual values?
- Moral values?
- Monetary values?
- Social values?
- Physical values?
- Societal values?
- Psychological values?

Use the information from those categories to create your power pedestal. You'll start to see what you want to keep and what you can discard. Maybe when you look at money, you write down that you never have enough. But then when you go back and think about it, that isn't true for you. You can find examples of times when you thought you wouldn't have enough, and then something happened, and you ended up having just what you needed. So maybe that changes from, "I never have enough" to, "I always have more than enough." See the difference?

Once you go back through and evaluate those values, you can start to rewrite them to fit who you are now. I'm going to take a wild guess and say that you won't write about obligation or sacrifice here if you're honest with yourself! It helps you see that you have a choice in how you want to live your life from now on. This may take more than one sitting to get through, and that's okay! Take all the time you need to honor your truth for each of the categories. With more clarity comes more strength when times get tough, and your values get challenged.

Here is an example: *I believe I can provide amazing value through my actions and thoughts to help other people achieve their goals in life. This value can be manifested in many ways, through my daily actions, how I interact with others, and what I put into the world as my work.*

How does that play out for me? Just because I'm living a life of service providing hope and guidance to others, does that mean that I give everything away for free? No. When I think about that, it doesn't match my monetary values.

When I'm helping others live their best lives, I believe that abundance is available to me as well as to them. There is a reciprocation happening. And I don't feel shame or guilt when a client asks for more than I can give them, and I have to turn down a request that doesn't align with what I see as my purpose work. I still have moments when I need to stop for a moment of reflection and ensure that my values are aligned to support my life path.

Once you decide all aspects of your power pedestal through those categories, you'll be less vulnerable to what other people say. The stronger you feel about yourself, the more confidence you have. Susceptibility to what others say will decrease and will decline! When you fully understand your value, it's amazing how things tend to roll off your back.

You begin to know when it's someone else's opinion and the filter of their own life experience, and they're projecting it upon you. It has nothing to do with you, and it has everything to do with them. And it's so much easier to let it go without taking what they say personally.

Consider this:

- Decide how you want to construct your values. And as you work through these, some thoughts and beliefs from other people are bound to show up.
- Does it resonate with you that you should attend parties and get-togethers out of obligation even if you really don't want to go?

- Do you believe that you have to sacrifice your time and work from sunrise to sundown to experience success?
- Take your time here and differentiate between what is yours and what isn't.
- What are you unequivocally unwilling to allow into your values?

When you see what you want to keep and what you want to discard, it's fun to have clarity on your core truth statement as a backup for when the going gets tough. Once you decide what your truth is, you're less vulnerable to what others say. The stronger you feel about yourself and the more confidence you have, the more susceptibility to what others say will decline.

I love when my clients have a moment of clarity and let me know that they went through their entire day and suddenly realized that the comment a friend made didn't affect them the way it would have, or a situation that would have freaked them out just came and went, and they realize how much they've grown. Put in the work and it can happen to you too!

My Reflections

I urge you to start calibrating yourself
to understand what's in your heart.

#LimitlessYou

Get Clear on Your Intentions.

Gratitude is one of the strongest and most transformative states of being. It shifts your perspective from lack to abundance and allows you to focus on the good in your life, which in turn pulls more goodness into your reality.
~ Jen Sincero

You understand how to lean in, and you see your meditation practice working, slowly but surely. You learned about the ways that your mind has been tricked and trapped over time, and you're filtering out what no longer serves you. Your power pedestal is ready for you to proclaim what you believe in proudly, and now it's time to set some goals and go after them. But first, understand that the intentions behind the actions you're about to take can make or break your goal-achieving success.

Often, intentions come from a place of lack or deprivation, so it's no wonder we fizzle out shortly after setting a goal, right? New Year's Resolutions become an afterthought halfway through January when you decide to just wait until the following year because you blew it those first two weeks.

We almost seep into sabotaging behaviors because the status quo seems preferential to getting out of our comfort zone and into something brand new. How can you set an excellent intention for yourself and put some feasible goals together to remain accountable or responsible? And then how can you move through it with sustainable energy and succeed in meeting those goals?

The last thing you want is to set a goal from negative thoughts.

For example, let's say I want to put some exercise goals into place. And I think, okay, I've got to lose this weight, I need to get 25 pounds off this frame. I'm already starting from a sense of less than! I'm looking at my body, and I'm feeling icky about myself. I don't have a sense of gratitude. I don't feel fulfilled. I'm just not feeling good. The mindset and the attitude make up the energy. Everything that we're putting into motion is going to be driven by them.

Do you feel like you're going to be very successful if you lead with something you don't like?

No. Of course not.

Most of the time, we feel like we're setting ourselves up for failure. And you think, "Well, if I don't achieve it, then I'm just a piece of garbage." Or "I know that I can't finish anything. It never works for me anyway, so I'm not going to set any goals this year." We start wrapping ourselves in those old traps and backing them up with this crappy attitude and send out our retriever brains to find those examples to prove ourselves right! And guess what? It will always find what we're looking for, whether it aligns with our truth or not.

How can you shift your focus on a direction where you can build a sustainable intention and move through it with exciting momentum? How can you develop an attitude and a perspective that supports the mindset to carry it through every day?

Most likely, you're going to be wanting to tap into a particularly emotional experience. Because that's what we are. We're human beings. Our attitudes, our emotions, our thoughts, and our belief systems drive us.

And so, how can you structure your life around supporting versus constantly working against yourself? It's time to stop feeling like you need to fight for your right to have a sense of peace and relaxation or grace and ease in your life.

You have to build it in. No one else is going to provide it for you. It's time to center your mind and your heart and become quiet in a place of self-reflection and sincerely ask, what is it that matters?

How much time are you awake in a day? Maybe 12 to 16 hours? What are you doing with that time? What kind of attitude are you exhibiting during the time that you have available every day? Does it match what matters to you on the inside? Or is it in complete contradiction of what you want to experience? Taking the way you spend your time and aligning it to your truth is how you start calibrating your life and moving things around.

Utilize your time in a way that you find that sense of satisfaction. Find points of gratitude, feel that sense of fulfillment, and live a life that you love. This is how you create the art of a limitless life! And it always, always, *always* boils down to some type of emotional experience.

Now consider your attitude when you think of the steps you want to take towards a new goal and what you're putting into motion because this will help you achieve success even quicker. It's almost like a quantum leap of collapsing time if you go about it with the right energy, attitude, and mindset.

For example, if I want to lose weight and think I'm going to exercise, that's an action step. I'm going to get out, and I'm going to run every day. We've always got to implement some sort of action steps to bring about that change.

When you set an action step, the intention behind the action makes all the difference. Check out the following examples.

I can get out there and start taking off running and jogging in a very self-defeating attitude with depleting energy. I can get out there and say, I've got to run because I have to work out this fat, and if I don't get fit, I'm just disgusting and ugly, and no one wants me, and my spouse will reject me. Or maybe I can't even get a spouse because I'm too heavy or too gross.

And I get out there, and I start putting that attitude into motion. I start running with this self-defeating outlook and perspective about myself. So not only am I putting negative energy into action, now I've attached it to my goal.

I'm probably going to get out there and start badgering myself with that inner critic in my mind on high alert. I start bringing in all the other reasons why I feel gross or down on myself.

People don't like me, or I can't have friends, or I can't get a spouse, or whatever the case may be. And so here I am. I'm generating more of that because I'm in motion now. Now I'm running, and now my mind's going wild with all kinds of negative thoughts. I'm getting meaner by the minute. My attitude is just spitting yucky stuff all over the place.

And now I have more of what I don't want. I'm running because I want to feel better about myself. Yet, I activated the momentum of all the unprofitable things, so I'm just throwing more fuel on my negative feelings. I end the run feeling worse than I did when I started. I decide there's no way it's worth it to do that again. And the goal dies, making me feel even worse.

So, how can you still take action with a different attitude and activate a new lens to view your world? Get a different mindset, and you have a fresh approach.

Let's try this again, shall we?

I jump out the door, and I start running. Because you know what? I love running! Maybe I don't even love running. Maybe I love that I'm allowing myself the opportunity to see if running is something I love. I can choose to achieve my goal if I just set my mind to it with the proper attitude and the appropriate amount of positive energy.

I look down and think about how grateful I am for the new running shoes I got last week. I appreciate my outfit choice because it's comfortable and soft on my skin as I pump my arms up and down while I run. Then I start having an appreciation for myself, like, Oh my gosh, good for me! And I'm looking around, seeing the birds, the trees, and other people exercising. I'm happy to surround myself with nature and feel like I'm a part of a larger community of runners.

And I've made it 13 seconds, and I'm out of breath. But I think *I'm doing it. I'm making it happen.* I keep moving forward, sometimes walking, sometimes running. A little smile tugs at the edges of my face as I feel the first bit of sweat bubbling up on my brow. I have a completely different outlook on it with a completely different energy and attitude.

Now I ask you, do you feel like I will achieve my goals that much more fluidly and quickly in the second example? I put appreciation, excitement, and exhilaration into motion. I experience feelings in myself like hope, faith, and trust. And I don't even know what's going to happen, but I'm doing something!

I'm trusting it. I'm putting myself out there. And as I start looking around, I'm connecting with nature, zeroing in on chipmunks and butterflies as I pass them. I'm just finding more and more things to be grateful for.

We get to share in the excitement and celebration with one another instead of saying, "Oh, I'm going to shrink down and play small because Betty Sue will judge me." Maybe this is your chance to inspire Betty Sue to set some goals of her own, just by honoring yourself and going after what you want in life. It can make such a difference!

Try this:

- When you look at your decisions, check on your attitude and the motivating factors behind them.
- Which three areas of your life need your attention and focus the most right now?
- How can you show up more fully as yourself?
- How can you allow that attitude to achieve whatever you want to translate and play out in your relationships?

Consider this:

- How can you support yourself in all areas of your life?
- Do you need to start speaking up in a gentler, kinder, more compassionate fashion with those around you?
- Do you need to stop shutting down, scared to death to say anything?
- What does that look like for you?

This is not an opportunity to say *I will tell you what I think* and then spit your aggression towards someone. Your chance is to truly honor all parts of you and honor others as well. It's a reciprocation of respect and a mutual playing out of really being in the same place, but also different places too. Isn't that amazing?

Because we all have a unique essence, and we can celebrate that in one another. I sincerely believe that we could all come together more cohesively and live through that unified front.

There's not so much separation of you versus me versus him versus her versus them versus us.

How can you bring the attitude of the kind of life you want to live through the lenses of unity? Look through the lenses of compassion, respect, and honor.

I guarantee you're going to activate a magnetizing force within you. More and more, you can find yourself in situations that will mirror that exact same attitude and energy. And you might find things starting to work out in this miraculous, magical way that you have no way to explain except that it started with you!

You shifted it by getting very clear with your intention and making the decisions that support it. And you chose to do it all with the right outlook, perspective, and attitude. Isn't that something more powerful we can lend our brothers and sisters across all of humanity? To say, "I am permitting myself to dream, and I invite you to do the same." And what would that look like for you? What do your dreams look like? What are they producing?

When you can master the gratitude behind the goals you set, you are on your way to embracing the art of a limitless life!

My Reflections

Your relationship with yourself sets the stage for any other relationship in your life.

#LimitlessYou

Create Your Support Systems.

Choose to focus your time, energy, and conversation
around people who inspire you, support you, and help
you to grow into your happiest, strongest, wisest self.
~ Karen Salmansohn

As you become more aligned with your soul, you'll start to notice changes in your life. There will come a time when you look back a few weeks, months, or even years and find yourself amazed at the changes that took place in the way you live your life and the opportunities that have shown up as a result of the work you've done.

To keep moving forward as you embrace this limitless life you're creating, you need to set some supports into place. Creating support systems can seem a bit tricky at first. And that's why we're going to look at two different types of support systems, both internal and external.

Let's look at your internal support system first.

Personal accountability is that sense of responsibility in you. Sometimes, it's that little voice inside of your head that says you need to do something. Don't think of it as your voice wagging a finger in your face, bossing you around. It's not about that. It's genuinely about bringing yourself back into a space that will carry you closer to your dreams, desires, wishes, and the life you want to live.

You're not just conducting yourself in these mindless habits day in and day out just to lay your head down on the pillow at night and think, oh, gosh, that day just completely wiped me out. Take responsibility to make the choices and set the intentions, so you can lay down at night thinking, oh, what a day! And I'm excited about tomorrow!

To get there, start by taking small steps forward. You can't get overwhelmed. Because then you start to think, oh my gosh, that's way too much! I can't do it. Look at yourself and ask, what can I do? What am I in charge of? And start putting those foundational pieces into place. How can you support yourself so that you can remain accountable for the things you want to change and focus on?

There is a difference between having control and taking charge of a situation. Sometimes you tell yourself to control this situation because you don't trust the outcome. It makes you feel like you need to micromanage and manipulate it to death to ensure that it does happen exactly the way you want it to happen.

Stand tall, stand firm, and stand in your power. Take one step and then another, moving with confidence. And even if you don't know what the heck you are doing, trust that you can figure it out! Take a step back and slide into the attitude and the disposition of taking charge.

You've always got to remember every single day that you are in the driver's seat of your life. So really ask yourself, what matters to me about who's driving, and what can I take charge of today? What is one area of my life that I can take charge of while I relinquish control and put my trust in what's on its way?

Let all your positive thoughts take up more space in your mind! Choose to think things like, "I've got this. I may not have all the answers, and I may not even have all the information yet, but I trust myself enough to get where I'm going and to figure it out!"

Position yourself to be fully accountable for your life, even when extraordinary circumstances show up. And I guarantee you. You're going to start noticing massive, monumental shifts in your life. But put on the lenses of desire to see the evidence of it. So that's how you can be your internal support system.

Let's talk about the support system around you.

These are your friends, your family members, and your colleagues. How are you showing up for yourself in those different dynamics? You need to be together in a position of collaboration instead of projection or expectation.

When you seek their external support, be mindful of the emotion you're putting into your intentions. Perhaps you go to a friend with thoughts of, "I'm so desperate, and you have to help me!" Do you see how that is asking from a place of lack and deprivation? How can you ask from a place of fully supporting yourself?

I know when I ask for external support to enter my world, it works because I'm already carrying that attitude. I'm taking that mindset. And I'm creating that thriving environment filled with the trust to keep moving forward and have fun in my world. Go ahead and bring some playful energy into your journey. Choose to trust yourself first. Then ask for external trust to enter your world that will support what you want.

How can you recalibrate your environment and the people around you to help you show up with positivity? When you get to that place, it truly does represent a support system! Not an expectation system, not a responsibility system, not an obligation system.

As human beings, we're always looking for inspiration outside of ourselves as we live our genuine self and our ultimate truth and allow others to feel that inside of themselves. But when we start shrinking down and catering to the needs of everyone around us, we're kind of setting ourselves up for a challenge, a conflict, and ultimately end up experiencing failure.

Sometimes we think that we're not brave. We believe that we're not courageous. But we all are. We could prevent those thoughts if we harness our power, live our truth, and tap into that inner courage.

Tap into your courage! Rely on your inner truth, set that first goal, and go for it with positive intentions and a support system in place.

Try this:

- Think about that first big goal that you want to see fulfilled. How will you show yourself that you support that dream coming true?
- Write down precisely what you want. Be as detailed and straightforward as you can!
- Give yourself a little positive mantra for those days when it feels impossible.
- Write down the names of two people who you trust to be the kind of supporters you need.
- Let them know how they can help you if you come to them with a setback or a celebration!
- Go after it wholeheartedly with those feelings of gratitude and trust that your dream is on its way because you believe in yourself!

Consider this:

- Don't move forward from a place of lack, desperation, fear, or criticism! Recalibrate yourself to inspiration, hope, appreciation, and gratitude. Work to make your attitude match the level of your dreams! Your dreams are not on the level of fear, rejection, or criticism.
- How can you ensure that you build a successful structure, so it moves further into a place of trusting and knowing that there can be no other way except this?

· Do you place the responsibility on others to ensure your happiness?

· Or is there a two-way street with equilibrium and an equal reciprocation of how you conduct yourself?

· Do you think your feelings of deprivation or fear are your soul's truth or a mind trick or trap popping up? Feel free to return to the first two chapters for some self-reflection and see what you notice.

Remember, you need that thriving environment for your dreams to reach you. Again, it's that two-way street. It's that reciprocation effect. You do this through your support system as well. That self-awareness comes with practice once you activate your soul.

My Reflections

As you hold yourself in that space of value,
other little things start lighting up again.
That beautiful clarity of insight.
Those instincts. That intuition.

#LimitlessYou

Cultivate Your Self-Awareness to Reconnect with Your Intuition.

There is a universal, intelligent life force that exists within everyone and everything. It resides within each of us as a deep wisdom, an inner knowing. We can access this wonderful source of knowledge and wisdom through our intuition, an inner sense that tells us what feels right and true for us at any given moment.
~ Shakti Gawain

I f you're ready to start tuning in and trusting your intuition, back up and practice self-awareness. You need to understand how to evaluate what's going on inside before getting back to where you hear your intuition and trust it enough to take action.

To me, self-awareness is like waking up and being an active participant in your life. It's not just falling victim to that chatter in your mind even when you're going through those everyday tasks.

Maybe you go to the store and start thinking, *oh well, I guess I better buy this shampoo because I'm broke as a joke, and I'll get this cheap brand off the shelf. I want the salon brand. Oh well, I guess that's just for the rich people anyways.* You never really take action to change the current set of circumstances that you're observing. Yes, they're real. Yes, you're in it. Yes, it's happening, but do you see how there's only a portion of you showing up to them?

Self-awareness is about activating all your physical senses and becoming aware of your whole self and your strengths. It's time to start cultivating the understanding that you can have something different if you want. You can *be* someone different if you wish.

Maybe your family members spoke about money from a place of lack. Did you ever hear things like, we can't afford it, money doesn't grow on trees, or something similar? Just because you heard it doesn't mean that is your ultimate truth.

I think the most significant power piece is that we get to choose our ultimate truth.

It's not chosen for us, although it very much seems that way. It may feel dictated or defined by whatever experiences you're observing or living through at the time. But that's not where it ends. That's just simply a state of awareness—one lens you can see it through. But if you choose to see things differently, you can respond differently, and then you get to act in accordance with what you want. Again, it's not just reacting to the world around you. Become proactive!

A significant first step to self-awareness was creating your power pedestal—now that you have a solid foundation to stand on, you need to remain abundantly clear on who you are from now on.

- How do you want to participate in the circumstances of your life?
- How do you want to interact with that family member or friend?
- How do you want to feel?
- Who do you want to be?

As humans, we tend to respond continuously and react to our environment. Typically, that's done through our emotional filters. We receive external messages all the time. And then, instead of living in the intuitive flow of your life, you find yourself scanning for the appropriate way to react and respond to things based on what you think other people want.

Something different occurs when you can take that step back and lean in thoughtfully. You find yourself contemplating what you need the most at that moment. You honor yourself when you can think and choose what feels most true to who you are before making a decision or engaging in a conversation.

It makes me think of a child who keeps asking why.

I was that kid. I think I drove everyone insane, but that's exactly the way my mind works!

I needed to understand why someone told me to do it that way, because what if there's a different way? A better way, a way that feels better for me, you know? So, I'd play their way and then decide if it's right for me or not. Then the questions and alternate ways to do it would start.

A part of self-awareness is activating more of your decision-making skills. When you align yourself to who you are and how you want to claim yourself as a person, not just again reacting and responding to your current set of circumstances in your life, your confidence is automatic.

You're the active participant when you're the one asking the questions and seeking those answers for yourself instead of just absorbing them from the world and society and even that internal voice.

It could have been your teacher from middle school who told you it always has to be this way, and it can never be any other way. And that's just the way it must be. Or your mother or your father telling you you're never going to amount to anything because nobody in your family ever has. Maybe no one's ever graduated from college, so you're just destined to be dumb. Do you know what I mean?

And you just kind of accept that as your ultimate truth because they've given you whatever they ran through their filter as some sort of external validation or evidence. But remember, they're looking at life through their retriever brain, and it's easy to follow along with those tricks and traps. You may see their point and the evidence they've gathered. It sounds like it makes logical sense, so you just make it your own and live according to that.

But what if you set it down?

And what if you just allowed them to have whatever thoughts they wanted to have, but you got to pick up something different?

You made a different selection off the shelf. What would that look like?

That's self-awareness. Start training yourself to use it! In the same way you exercise to build muscles, you must activate and understand it through your senses. And as you strengthen your self-awareness, your intuition will inevitably begin to show up more and more.

Trust me. It took a lot of work to get to this point in my life. Something would come at me, and I'd make a snap judgment and create a story around the event. Then I'd spend hours going back over the conversation, analyzing my every move to try and make myself believe it was the right choice.

I became somewhat disconnected from my intuition. I'd feel something and ignore it because it wasn't true to who I was and how I responded to my environment during that period of my life.

I'd think things like:

- I can't listen to my intuition right now because if I acted on it, this person would think this about me.
- That person will negatively receive me.
- So let me just shove that down and look around for the answers.
- I'll just go along with what everyone else thinks I should do based on who they are instead.

I'd work to find the "appropriate and socially acceptable" answer and do that. But something in me knew it wasn't my truth. I felt disconnected from myself. I was severely dissatisfied with my choices.

It was almost like a painful soul nudge trying to remind me of who I really was deep down, and then this hole in my heart would deepen as I'd wake up the next day and find myself living through the same cycle all over. It was exhausting to exert the effort to go against my true self and then validate what felt "off" from the jump.

No matter how much I analyzed a situation, self-doubt filled me. I'd sit alone, wringing my hands with my gut bubbling, worrying that whatever just happened didn't sit well with whomever I interacted with. My intuition created a physiological reaction to the experience, trying to get my attention and tell me, *wait a minute! I don't think this is in alignment with you!*

I needed to go back through my days and evaluate my alignment to my choices. But I didn't understand how. I wasn't clear about who I was, so I couldn't correctly do any kind of self-evaluation without that foundation in place.

I urge you to go back into Chapter Eight if you didn't already create your power pedestal. It's imperative to know who you are and what you stand for as you grow on this journey.

When I chose to take the time to invest in myself, it was so freeing. I started to understand my value. And as I became more valuable, my life became more and more fulfilling.

My intuition became alive again. It didn't just become alive. It was *thriving,* baby! It had its own heartbeat. One of my favorite realizations at that point in my life was the fact that all the anxious thoughts I'd become so used to lose their grip when my intuitive voice became clear.

All the thoughts began to quiet down and then leave me alone:

- Should I or should I not do that?
- What if this?
- What if that?
- Did I react appropriately at that moment?

I had this new beautiful dance with myself. The words presented themselves. The solutions came. Now, that doesn't mean that I didn't act. It means that as I evaluated the information coming from my internal wisdom, I no longer needed to seek outside cues.

When you value and honor yourself to the point that you deeply listen to that inner voice, you truly become alive on a whole different level!

If you're constantly letting everyone else's opinions, thoughts, and projections drive you, you're just used to that tone, and typically it's very defeating. It's telling you all the things that you're not. It's telling you all the things that you can't do. It's telling you everything you should be doing better because you're inferior now, right?

That isn't the case with your intuition.

It acts as your inner advocate! You're not always getting sparkly messages that come down from the heavens on rainbows, but it could even be that nudge that says, you know what? Make that doctor's appointment. Something is going on in your body that needs your attention right now. And a lot of people translate that and think, oh my gosh, I'm just overreacting.

There's something fearful when you jump up into your head-space, but intuition is just clear data. You can get tangled up when you let your brain try to analyze that clear data. But when you are self-aware, you can receive more explicit messages.

Remember that telephone game where a message goes through this person, that person, and so on until it's so contorted that by the time it gets to you, it makes no dang sense, and you laugh when you go back and see what the actual message was? Intuition without having the self-awareness to discern between it and the tricks and traps can feel a lot like that game. Sometimes it's easier to forget the message altogether and move on. Understand, getting to that place isn't something that's just going to come overnight. However, we were absolutely born with it.

There is at least one example for every human being alive, and it doesn't matter what life looked like for you. You've at least had one moment of vivid clarity when you *just knew* something.

Maybe it's a person that you looked at and knew something felt off about them. You're not judging that person. You do not fear that person. It's simply information. It is raw data that is coming through you and for you.

It's very easy to start wrapping the emotions around it. That's where it goes from clear raw data to a personal entanglement. And that is when you can call on your self-awareness to calm those stories down.

Intuition can be as simple as thinking of calling someone and getting a call from them a few minutes later or getting a little *yes* immediately when that job offer shows up in your inbox.

You're interacting more with yourself than you are responding to your environment. And you start to get the information you need, which will best serve you to react and interact with your environment because you're interacting with *yourself* first. You're not placing everything else outside of you.

Self-awareness doesn't happen overnight.

I'm not expecting you to wake up tomorrow, snap your fingers, and have all the clarity you need! There are too many tricks and traps that you'll dig through and release over time. But the good news is that you are more self-aware just by reading the previous chapters.

You understand the idea of creating false positives, and you know that some emotional reactions can come from unresolved events from the past and not the present. But it's time to start creating your self-evaluation discipline, here and now.

There's a difference between a task, an activity, and discipline. Practicing your self-awareness is a discipline. It isn't something you do out of obligation. You do it because you are working to hear your truth and then live it with passion!

Bring that inner kid out. The one that's the never-ending questioner. Start asking yourself:

- Why do I have to do it like that?
- Why do I have to wear this?
- Why do I have to say it this way?

Listen closely to your answers to strengthen those self-aware-ness muscles. You may even start to hear your ultimate truth in them. And then come the intuitive thoughts.

Try this:

At the end of each day, ask yourself if you valued and honored yourself in the following categories:

- Mind
- Emotions
- Energy
- Body
- Heart
- Belief System (I mean your belief in your infinite potential here!)

Consider this:

When you honor your intuition, you become the extraordinary leader of your life.

How will your life change when you see yourself as:

- Intuitive?
- Capable?
- Passionate?
- Filled with a zest for life?

When you run into external issues, the faith in yourself that you've built up over time will help you move through those sit-uations in a way that honors and values who you are.

Because guess what?

You are an amazing human being who deserves the right to live your truth! Once you get there, it becomes automatic. And then one day, you'll look back amazed at how far you've come!

Your mind is open to the truth
about self-imposed limits.
You are stronger than the illusion.

#LimitlessYou

Nurture Your Truth and Practice Playfulness.

Trust yourself. Create the kind of self that you will be
happy to live with all your life. Make the most
of yourself by fanning the tiny, inner sparks
of possibility into flames of achievement.
~ Golda Meir

A s humans, we're constantly seeking out certainty. We hold ourselves back from experiences when we can't see the absolute guarantee that it ends with our expected outcome. But you've learned a lot about yourself and the things you value most in life. You're beginning to trust the process toward living your life without limits.

The more you can use your internal guidance system to keep you on track from now on, the better. By working on your self-awareness surrounding your power pedestal and inner truth, you simultaneously strengthen your relationship with certainty. And the stronger that relationship becomes, the easier it is for you to trust your decisions and eliminate self-doubt. How great will it be when you catch yourself going an entire week/month/year without questioning your choices?

When you know your power pedestal, you know your truth. And then you can stand on that deep understanding of who you are and everything you stand for that comes from within. With your inner and outer support systems, you know how to get that encouragement when you need it. And you can always revert to that ultimate sense of knowing from within.

Let's look at my power pedestal example:

I came here to be seen and have a profound impact on the world. It is my ultimate privilege, pleasure, and responsibility to live through the fullness of my presence and pull in that visibility wherever I go, through the frequencies of compassion, honor, and truth.

I can always go back and rely on it as I move throughout my days. And when I notice something happening that doesn't match that power pedestal, I can take some time for self-reflection before the situation takes me down a path that doesn't match the life I say I want to live.

When you're working to live in your truth, invite in some playfulness.

Think about it. You're confused about a situation or decision. You don't want to get all serious all over again. So why not get back to your truth in a light-hearted way that can lift your spirits?

Maybe you get a tune in your mind, and you create your cliche. If you were watching a movie with some music playing in the background, what would those lyrics be for a character going through the challenge or obstacle you're going through? Would you hear the song, Don't Stop Believing? Or visualize the poster of a kitten holding onto a tree branch that says Hang In There? Can you think of one that makes you roll your eyes and chuckle? That automatically changes the emotion your brain is zeroed in on when you can shift it towards a positive emotion instead.

Think about watching someone walking through the park with his head down. He's letting his feet drag through the dirt, and his shoulders slump in sadness. Maybe he needed to feel it for that moment to just kind of discover something about himself. But then he recalls a peppy song, and he starts running along the grass as his feet hit the ground to the beat in his mind, ready to take on the day.

As I said before, your emotions need to move through your body. They're not supposed to stay buried within. That's why you must get the experience of all of them so they can move through you and move on.

When you bring forth a playful way to shift your thinking, you're creating new mental pictures, so you don't start to let yourself sink into the same old patterns. When you lived with all the tricks and traps, your brain was firing on that same loop for years, maybe even decades.

But by bursting into song or engaging in that youthful energy, you're interrupting the loop from continuing to go further, and you are re-calibrating a new circuit in your brain. So, the more you reinforce it, the stronger that circuit becomes, and your brain goes through a natural pruning process. Your neuro-circuitry in your brain is changing.

Every 60 days, your brain implements an internal scan. It determines which circuits are the strongest, and it allows them to continue to fire. Have you ever heard the phrase what wires together fires together? Or if you don't use it, you lose it? When you feel upset and choose to be silly to change how you're feeling, you're changing your wiring so those circuits in your brain fire differently. And when they do, that's your way of literally changing your mind to change your life. *How cool is that?*

Keep in mind that you fuel your attitude with your emotions and energy, which powers the mind's activity. How often do you tell yourself a story then start getting really fired up about it? You start thinking, "Oh that stupid woman did this thing to me, and I should have told her this, and I should have told her that." And now it's just as real as it was when you experienced the encounter and you've got this feeling like you want to go after her all over again, right?

You put so much emotion behind it, and now that story is super alive. Those circuits are firing. In the process, you feel defeated or disempowered and angry, and all the things. And as you reinforce that same circuit, the stronger it gets. The more you believe it, the more real it becomes.

Then you begin to observe more and more of those experiences because your retriever brain thinks, *oh, you believe that to be your absolute truth? Cool, let me find something to prove you right*. And then comes the day when you wonder why everyone around you is so irritating. That is why it's so important to adjust your attitude and take the time to check in with yourself to live your truth without spiraling out of control with negative thoughts.

When you go into your playful mode, you're activating your right brain.

It's more visual and more intuitive by nature because it's less organized. Your left brain is where all the analytics are. But when you're activating that right brain, you're moving into more creative forces. It's such an awesome shortcut you can use to tap into deeper levels of your intuition!

Intuition won't fit into the logic because it's less organized. It may not have any kind of physical evidence to back it up, because it's more about listening to your truth and trusting the path that you are on. You're moving into more random and intangible ideas. Your right brain responds to music tones, lyrics, and things like that. So, when you're trying to pivot your mood or shift your attitude, you're moving out of that linear brain and into the more playful and artistic side.

When you understand that your brain can change, you can consciously break through those old patterns. Or, like my momma used to say, get an attitude adjustment. It's fascinating to know that the way your brain works isn't permanent! Allowing yourself to shift into a better mood moves you up on the emotional scale of awareness.

I don't typically listen to pop music, but a while back, when I heard one of Katy Perry's songs, those lyrics touched my soul.

I remember listening closely to the questions in that song thinking, *yeah, sometimes I **do** feel like that paper bag! Dang, Katy, you're on point, girl!*

Try this:

- Start paying attention to the lyrics in songs. Which songs give you the chills? Lean into the lyrics and pay attention to the emotions that come with those lyrics.
- Start to create your power playlists.
- Create one filled with songs that pump you up and make you want to sing and dance as soon as they start playing.
- Create another one with songs that make you feel calm and happy.
- Grab some sticky notes and write down some of your favorite empowerment cliches or quotes, then stick them inside your desk at work, in your car's glove box, or on your bathroom mirror.

Consider this:

On a day when you're running mundane errands, decide to be the music director of your movie. You want the audience to see your character go from defeated to empowered. Think about what you'll play in the background when:

- You walk out to the car and step in dog poop.
- You drive, and someone cuts you off.
- You get to the first store, and they're out of what you wanted.

- The lines are long.
- You see a dear friend in the parking lot.
- She compliments your earrings.
- At the next store, they have everything you need.
- The lines are short.
- You find out everything you picked up is on sale.

Playfulness helps you find a different rhythm. When you activate the right side of your brain, you have other solutions made available to you versus being on that more logical and analytical left side. When you live in your truth, your intuition gets clearer. You're activating your right brain now to respond to more imagination and get into that intuitive flow.

Remember, you have a choice
in the face of fear.
Believe in the fear OR
have faith in yourself.

#LimitlessYou

Resistance is Not Futile.

The more important a call to action is to our soul's
evolution, the more Resistance we will feel about answering
it. But to yield to Resistance deforms our spirit. It stunts us
and makes us less than we are and were meant to be.
~ Steven Pressfield

You're on your way to choosing to live in your truth. Congratulations! Just know that at some point, you'll feel like you're hitting a glass ceiling or an upper limit. Think of this journey as though you're climbing a ladder. And as you ascend rung by rung, you run into different characters. These characters aren't just random people. They're actually different versions of yourself, but they represent old tricks and traps that have held you back in the past.

It's time to learn how to handle those difficult situations as you are changing and growing into the life you want to live.

Instead of getting to a point where you look around and have no idea how you got into such a mess, you now know how to lean in and listen to what you need to care for yourself the most at any moment. This will help you prevent the confusion and chaos that can occur when meaningful change occurs.

As soon as you recognize shut-down mode creeping in, immediately refer to a song on your power playlist or one of those silly things that help you shift away from that old way of thinking. Then your brain automatically starts reinforcing that new circuit that you've already created.

It becomes stronger and stronger. Then finally, you're thinking, *dang, I got this.*

If you usually shut down and go to your bedroom to hide under the covers, put a note there. Think of a great message you could ask yourself, like, *hey, do you really want to shut down right now?* Or if you're feeling sassy, it could say, *I love you, so get your booty out of this bed right now!* It's great to have some kind of cue to remind yourself that you're working on breaking a pattern that no longer serves you but try your best to keep it light and playful. There is no room for guilting or shaming yourself into action (remember to stay mindful of positive intentions). You always have the power to choose another way that moves you closer to your truth.

When you're moving through one of those upper levels, you're moving into new territory.

You're moving from the familiar comfort into a space full of new experiences, and that is when you start to hit some resistance.

And your retriever brain doesn't have any evidence to indicate that this new territory is safe or has any element of certainty.

Be careful here, because you'll start to experience those "f-words" (fight, flight, faint, or freeze). In those moments, take a deep breath and remind yourself that moving out of your comfort zone and into new territory naturally activates this part of your brain, but that doesn't make it your ultimate truth.

Maybe it's the trap that you simply aren't good enough because every time you exerted yourself as a child in some manner, someone else acted as if you just didn't measure up to their standards. When that happens, you create an identity based on someone else's opinion and their translation of your output. Then that led you to the trap that your work equals your value. Essentially, these glass ceilings are just a place you've built up in your mind.

You start hearing those old tricks in your mind:

- I'm not good enough.
- I'm not ready for this.
- People are going to do this or say that if I try this.

Remember, having a thought doesn't necessarily make it your ultimate truth.

This is fear talking. It could be the fear of being seen, losing love and connection, not being good enough, or any combination of fears that got shoved down over time. Dig them up, address them, and let them go. Go back to Chapters five and six whenever you need a refresher.

You've put in a lot of work up to this point. I'm so proud of you! Now let's take that momentum and look at making changes in your life. Just keep reminding yourself that when resistance shows up in your life, it's actually a sign of progress. You're moving out of your comfort zone and into new uncharted territory. Trust me, resistance is a good thing!

You have that soul nudge:

- It's time to move.
- This relationship is over.
- Apply for that other job.

But another part of you thinks about how big and scary it is to act on that choice. How do you go from hearing your intuition to acting on it? It sounds so cliche, but you're going to get there one step at a time. When you commit to honoring your inner healing and growth, your confidence strengthens. Keep referring to the chapters you're led to when you feel stuck and see what jumps out. It always surprises me when I reread a favorite book and I get an entirely new insight that I didn't get the first time around.

Lean in when appropriate and engage your creativity and playfulness when you notice your emotions taking a dip. Listen to your intuition and write down one goal that seems to keep showing up. But don't stop there. Create a list of the things that don't honor who you are in that particular space.

If you're ready to change jobs, your list may consist of thoughts like:

- I don't like this job anymore.
- I don't feel like I belong here.
- I don't appreciate the way the boss treats me.
- I'm ready to try something new.

Lean in and ask yourself why you believe each of those statements to be true. Maybe you don't feel like they listen to you anymore. Or you feel defeated or disempowered. Take the time to recognize all the areas that are incongruent with your power pedestal.

Remember how your brain likes certainty? Well, I guarantee that your power pedestal is not interested in a job that leaves you feeling defeated and undervalued all day, every day.

If you're feeling undervalued and defeated all the time, how do you combat that and counteract it?

You might be thinking, wow, I must be the worst employee alive if this is how he's treating me. But is that the truth? Or is he just projecting his issues onto you? If you're doing your best and you're contributing to the best of your ability, and it's still not equating to a place where you feel valuable, it's time to ask yourself why you're relying on someone else's validation or opinion in the first place.

This is the internal work that you must do. In those moments, activate more of that right brain. Do something creative that makes you feel that sense of pure joy. Something that makes you think, wow, I value my time right now. I love my energy. I appreciate my body. I value my relationships. I value my family.

How are you using the attitude of honoring yourself and exhibiting that value? When you look at the situation from the perspective of honoring yourself, you become more confident in your decision. It's not as scary because then it boils down to letting yourself wonder, would I want to stay somewhere when these guys treat me like dirt? Where's the honor in that? Forget this. I'm out.

It feels incredible when you can finally hear yourself thinking, I'm no longer allowing or accepting this type of behavior. I find myself to be more valuable, and I love myself more than being someone's doormat for one more moment. The more you conjure up that energy of value within, the more you become in alignment with your truth.

And perhaps another opportunity comes into your life when you're not looking for it in a way that feels desperate, urgent, or needy. Instead, you go at it thinking, man, I'm so excited to have a job where I feel heard and valued every day!

You put resumes out, you go for interviews, you talk to friends and family, but you're not freaking out and scrambling around thinking, oh my gosh, is anybody hiring? You don't jump at the first help wanted sign just to have some kind of job. You realize it's because those old ways aren't firing anymore. You're no longer taking this kind of nonsense for face value.

Keep in mind, not everyone is working on learning about who they are, where they stand without any outside influence or coming back to understanding how to lean in and follow their intuition. As you grow, you may meet new people on a similar path and create new friendships. But at the same time, some old friendships may come to an end.

If you notice some awkwardness or withdrawal from co-workers, friends, or even family members, it's another sign that you're becoming a more authentic version of yourself. They may not have ever seen the real you! Be honest and open about your journey to self-awareness. They may feel inspired and choose to work on themselves. They may see something in you that they don't think they can find within, and it could make them uncomfortable with the real you. Or any number of reactions.

Just remember that whatever happens, if you come from a place of honoring yourself and others as you address these encounters, you can walk away knowing that you're doing what is best for you to live your truth. There is no need for shame or guilt when some people grow apart.

You're deciding from within what your value is, what you choose to be like, and who you are at your core. What you want and what you choose to experience, and what you decide to become. You don't just take someone else's word for it. Then you find the situations, people, and circumstances in your external environment to match what you have on the inside. If it does not fit, then you know it's not for you. Discernment isn't selfish. It's actually a great way to love and honor yourself. So go ahead and love yourself enough to get picky about your life!

Think about this:

Ready for another cliche? Whether you win or lose, it's all in how you play the game. So how are you playing the game of life? It's time to start looking at life from the perspective of your inner winner's attitude.

- Are you living with desperation, needy, and urgent thoughts, feelings, and behaviors?
- Do you refer to your inner critic and choose to beat yourself up every day?
- Or are you choosing to love, honor, and value yourself as you play?
- Are you finding the fun in the little things?
- Can you see your potential from within?
- Are you moving out of your comfort zone and into your All-star phase?

Consider this:

Get very clear on a goal that you're moving towards or one where you find yourself hesitating as you get closer to achieving it. Maybe you're on that ladder, and the next rung feels out of reach. You may even feel yourself physically shrinking back and contracting from that place of fear.

- Look at your thoughts, behaviors, and actions and start to ask some questions.
- Is this a reaction? Or am I living my life proactively?
- Is this coming from me, or is it a reflection of someone else's tricks and traps?
- Are the conflicts with my decision-making coming from my intuition or an old fear that no longer serves me?
- Am I too hard on myself?
- Am I pressuring myself?
- Is that old perfectionism taking over?
- How can I shift my thoughts at this point of choice?

Take those answers into account and decide whether your thoughts, behaviors, and actions move you closer to or further from your truth. You can pull your power back and create the reality that supports you by tapping into the potential that has been there all along, just under the surface.

And that, my friend, is how you begin to embrace the art of a limitless life!

Stay strong in your beliefs, values,
and your commitment to healing.
Start creating the EPIC life you deserve!

#LimitlessYou

Acknowledgments

I would like to thank anyone and everyone who has come in and out of my life, graced me with their presence, or maybe even triggered me to bring me to a broader and deeper understanding of myself, thus birthing this book. As I reflect on all of my friends and family and loved ones, I can see, and truly hold each of you in a very special place with my heart.

To my beloved husband for endlessly being my cheerleader and supporting me every step of the way.

I want to thank my best friend Samantha for loving my family as if it was your own. Meeting you on the day that I gave birth to my daughter, makes it even more special. Thank you for always being there for me, Sam. I love you always.

To my incredible clients who trust me so I can watch you grow and flourish into the magical beings that you were always meant to be.

To my mother for demonstrating love, even in the toughest times.

To my incredible grandparents who showed me how to live my own way, laugh, and enjoy the company of others. And my precious Nana, you were the embodiment of unconditional love.

To my darling children who reflect anything and everything I need to further activate and heal within myself to become the wholesome being I'm always aligning to become.

My precious pup, Mojo. My Best Boy, you've been my rock. In the hardest times you were with me and helped me make it through.

To Dr. Paulson, for believing in me and showing me that I was truly gifted in terms of pursuing the path of psychology. And the many mentors and coaches that allowed me to uncover even more of those gifts so I can bridge psychology with the incredible energy methods that formulate my magic touch.

My dad, even though I only had you for a couple of years before you left this world, because without you I would not be here.

Last but surely not least, my two brothers, one still walking the planet and one that left too soon. To Kevin, for always showing me how to laugh and reminding me how to take it easy. Kurt Burt, you're forever in my heart. And because of him, I really lunged into this book wholeheartedly. Message after message he gave me, pushing me to do this. And bringing this book to its perfect completion, on the anniversary of his parting is serendipitous at the very least. It's pretty cool!

And finally, thank you for the ones who allowed me to pick their brains for this process and use their awesome skills to help bring this book to life. Tracy, Kristin, and Julie, I love you all so much.

Love and Light to you all,

Holly

About the Author

Holly Wynn is a board-certified empowerment coach through the Association of Integrative Psychology. She has dedicated her life's work to learning the ins and outs of the human psyche through her degrees in traditional psychology, certifications in Neuro-Linguistic Programming, Hypnotherapy, REBT Coaching, Law of Attraction Coaching and trainings with the Heart Math Institute, amongst many others. Her spiritual approach weaves methods from her certifications as a Reiki Master Teacher, Theta Healer, and Empowered Energetics Practitioner and Trainer to bring her clients to an empowered level of consciousness, with practical real-life application. With this lifelong thirst to help others evolve into the best versions of themselves, Holly mentors clients as a Trauma Informed Care Practitioner, with behavior re-patterning through Rational Emotive Behavior Therapy Coaching with Intuition Development. She helps her clients dig deep into finding their authentic potential by defining the root origin of their thought patterns, emotional triggers, and behavioral cycles to discover emotional freedom. Holly currently lives her dream life with her husband, Danny and her 2 youngest children on land filled with animals in Georgia. She is pursuing her certification in Yoga Psychology, developing Oracle Wisdom Cards, and writing her next book.

Explore More

I f you enjoyed this journey and would like to dive in for more and stay up to date on my new releases, jump on over to iamhollywynn.com. There are always courses, meditations, and trainings available for you to continue your personal development journey.

A free ebook edition is available with the purchase of this book.

To claim your free ebook edition:

1. Visit MorganJamesBOGO.com
2. Sign your name CLEARLY in the space
3. Complete the form and submit a photo of the entire copyright page
4. You or your friend can download the ebook to your preferred device

MorganJames BOGO™

A **FREE** ebook edition is available for you or a friend with the purchase of this print book.

CLEARLY SIGN YOUR NAME ABOVE

Instructions to claim your free ebook edition:
1. Visit MorganJamesBOGO.com
2. Sign your name CLEARLY in the space above
3. Complete the form and submit a photo of this entire page
4. You or your friend can download the ebook to your preferred device

Print & Digital Together Forever.

Snap a photo

Free ebook

Read anywhere

Printed in the USA
CPSIA information can be obtained
at www.ICGtesting.com
JSHW022142160124
55462JS00006B/60